UNDERSTANDING MEZCAL

James Schroeder

prensa press

UNDERSTANDING MEZCAL

James Schroeder

Understanding Mezcal

Published by Prensa Press
Mexico City, Mexico · Chicago, IL
www.prensa.press

Book design by Polly Jiménez
Edited by Paul Biasco
Science Editor Ivan Gonçalves Ribeiro, PhD.

For more information contact: info@prensa.press

First hardcover edition December 2018
Printed in India

ISBN 978-0-692-17108-0 (hardcover)

By James Schroeder

To Mildred Weber, whose compassion, love, and unrelenting tenacity will be with me always.

Preface

The story of mezcal is beautiful and inspiring. In contemporary life, far too many of us live a life largely removed from the perceptible influence of history and tradition. Mezcal is a story. It is a breathing example of people and places. Mezcal is a tangible product, but it is fundamentally inseparable from the individuals who make it. Their stories inform their wares and heighten our enjoyment of something that's already undeniably delicious.

Often mezcal is written about from the perspective of story and anecdote. At best, these anecdotes center around those who create mezcal and whose traditions we get to enjoy in liquid form. Other times they center around the role of the author and their tales of encounters with the people and places that make mezcal happen. While one could make a strong argument that maybe mezcal never needed to be discovered, this element of encounter is one that is often easy to relate to for those living outside the world of mezcal production.

Readers of mezcal books are a strange subset of the universe: curious newcomers, the experienced mezcal consumers, various beverage-industry soldiers on the front lines, and the seasoned bar professionals. The latter may have many subjects other than mezcal clamoring for their attention. There is one common thread that unites all of the above—curiosity and mild terror.

The mezcal travelogue narrative satisfies our well-deserved sense of wonder at this category and its potential to appeal broadly to consumers on a world stage. It allows us to live vicariously through a well-traveled person's discovery of a culture and the culture's endemic beverage which existed in much its same form well before the intrepid author's grandparents were born. The stories and anecdotes these tales contain coax the reader to approach the category of mezcal with appropriate deference. *There's this thing, it's beautiful, I want to learn about it, and I want to share what I've learned with others so they can appreciate it too.*

Most literary efforts surrounding mezcal also endeavor to address the technical aspects of the process. One can not merely mention a clay pot still without first explaining what it is, or for that matter, what a still is in general. While these works are well menaning and often well written, they generally take two approaches in broad strokes. The first is to look at the generalities of production, but not dig too deep. In that approach, you, the reader, get the gist and it's assumed the blanks need not be filled in. The other method is a bit more absolutist—this works this way, and always results in that.

The truth is, the world of mezcal is exactly like the real world, beset by shades of gray on all sides.

This book sets out with a different purpose in mind, one that may end up being ill-advised. What this work attempts to do is hopefully as useful as it is decidedly un-sexy. It spares the romance for those with far better literary skills than I. This work sets out with the primary goal of giving the reader something practical. You, reader, are to go forth and use the thoughts and ideas contained herein. We will look at the nuts and bolts that create the liquid, the plants that make it possible, and the forces that shape the market in which we actively participate.

The time of writing for this work is the Year of our Lord 2019. Prognostication is generally an excellent way to make oneself look rather foolish, but I can say with certainty that no matter what shape it takes, the market for mezcal will look very different in five years time. The forces placed on that market will directly affect how it will look in 2024 and beyond. The number one driving force has been and will always be the folks shelling out their hard-earned money for mezcal. You.

Mediocre and mass-produced products are already flooding the market, aiming to prey on both a general lack of education among consumers and those same consumers' raw enthusiasm. I say with great pride that the current mezcal consumer is voracious in their appetite to know more about this esoteric spirit. This book aims to aid in their pursuits of knowledge.

Mezcal is seeing its world debut at a time when the craft movement has touched everything from farming to hand soap. Craft beer was once scoffed at by multinational corporations. Now, breweries are acquired by the behemoths and passed around like trading cards. Where there is money to be made, corporate America will not fear to tread.

There is no doubt we will see the same tricks played in the mezcal market as are played elsewhere in Late Capitalism—celebrity endorsements, advertising saturation, and aggressive marketing to bar-folks and consumers. We will also see pay-to-play tactics at your favorite

Upstanding Local Independent Craft Cocktail Bar. At times, influence is a result of good intention or being friends with a charismatic brand rep, but you'd be surprised at what some are willing do for a free trip to Mexico. To prevent the category of mezcal from developing into something soulless or exploitative, we're going to have to pay close attention to the what and the why of brands and the intentions of the folks behind them.

This is why you're here, dear reader. And I'm glad to be here with you. Maybe ten years from now we'll have a beer alongside a small glass of something stashed away long ago and lament the State of Mezcal 2029. The very least we can do is educate the crap out of ourselves and try our damnedest to be the loudest, most demanding, nerdiest, and most well-intentioned spirits drinkers on the planet. I fancy myself very much the pragmatist in life, but I'll be damned if I don't fight tooth-and-nail for what I believe in, even if it means I'm not best buddies with the big-box multinational mezcal brands that have more money than I'd even know what to do with. Your boy has come way too far and believes in this category way too much to sell out.

A final note: I've been advised by various influential people and savvy literary insiders not to follow my educational pursuits as I have, and not to write this exact book which you hold. To them, I owe genuine gratitude. Detraction has sufficiently fueled my contrarian streak and given me the nudge I needed to create the exact thing I envisioned.

They also may turn out to be right. Glossy cocktail books are quite the thing. Maybe I've spread myself too thin in my continuing personal journey towards understanding mezcal. Regardless, I stand by this work and hope you, dear reader, find in it a great deal of utility.

Mezcal as a Term

Before we get started, we need to do a bit of housekeeping. For hundreds of years, the term mezcal has been used as a generic category term for spirits made from the agave plant. This pertains to the known and established category of tequila, as well as all other forms of agave spirits all over Mexico. They all fit into one big happy mezcal family, with some spirits finding and laying claim to their own regional identities and names within that family. The term mezcal finds its origins in the Nahuatl terms for cooked agave, and its roots likely stretch back to a time where cooked agave was an important source of food in Mesoamerica.

In 1994 a Denomination of Origin was created defining mezcal as a specific category of spirits. A denomination of Origin is a legal means by which a country can protect one of its indigenous products from counterfeiting or copycats. Think of it as an international trademark for a type of product. DOs exist all over the world, and their purviews generally extend over the realms of food, beverage, and agricultural products. DOs generally regulate not just where something can come from, but also the process by which the product is made. In order for Champagne to be Champagne, it must both be from Champagne France and be made in the style of Champagne.

DOs in Mexico are governed by sets of rules, known as NOMs. In 1994 NORMA Oficial Mexicana NOM-070-SCFI-1994 set out the terms for the mezcal DO and defined the word 'mezcal' as a protected product name which could only be created in certain geographical locations within Mexico and which had to conform to specific production standards. As far as the Mexican government was concerned, mezcal was now a specific thing from a specific place. The NOM set out that mezcal could only be produced in 8 Mexican states. In 1995 the world obliged, and mezcal became a protected term in Mexico and abroad. Meanwhile, in Estado de México, rural Jalisco, and in enclaves all over Mexico, traditional producers carried on producing what they referred to as mezcal and didn't pay the law much mind. As long as these smaller producers sold locally and did not attempt to market their products beyond their communities, their existence was of little importance to the newfound DO and its economic interests.

The first NOM standards and the mezcal DO represented a major paradigm shift. The goals of the DO were multifold. On the positive side, they were rudimentary attempts to lay out production standards and to guarantee some protection to traditional mezcal producing practices. On the negative side, they drew a line in the sand geographically and restricted the use of a formerly-generic term to only mean one specific thing. Imagine someone trying to create a DO for the term 'whiskey' or 'sparkling wine.' It wouldn't go over so well. That line in the sand also ostensibly limited the people and communities to whom the financial benefits of an international mezcal industry would flow. If you weren't in one of those eight states, you could not legally export your product as a mezcal. Finally, the DO and NOM standards paved the way for a lucrative regulatory industry to grow and thrive. To legally produce mezcal, producers must have their production sites certified and must pay to certify each batch of mezcal they make.

What does this mean for our terminology? Before, all tequila was mezcal, but not all mezcal was tequila. At present, all mezcal is mezcal, and all tequila is tequila. The only bucket into which both can fit is the not-nearly-as-catchy-sounding category of 'agave spirits.' We can love it or hate it, but in the eyes of the law, mezcal means something much more specific than it used to.

Since 1994 the mezcal DO has continued to grow in power and purview. At this moment, mezcal can now be legally made in nine Mexican states, and there is more certified mezcal being produced right now than ever before. As we embark on our journey to learn about mezcal, this leaves us with a serious quandary: what does the word 'mezcal' even mean?

Annoyingly, there is no easy answer. This work at times uses the term 'mezcal' and the newfound category name 'agave spirits' interchangeably. At others, it uses the term to refer specifically to the DO process and certified product known as mezcal. The long and short of it is that outside the actual certification process, the concerns of those producing mezcal within the DO or outside its realm are pretty much identical and can be looked at in parallel. As we go along I'll try to lay it out as clearly as possible, but remember we're working with concepts that are just a bit confusing at times.

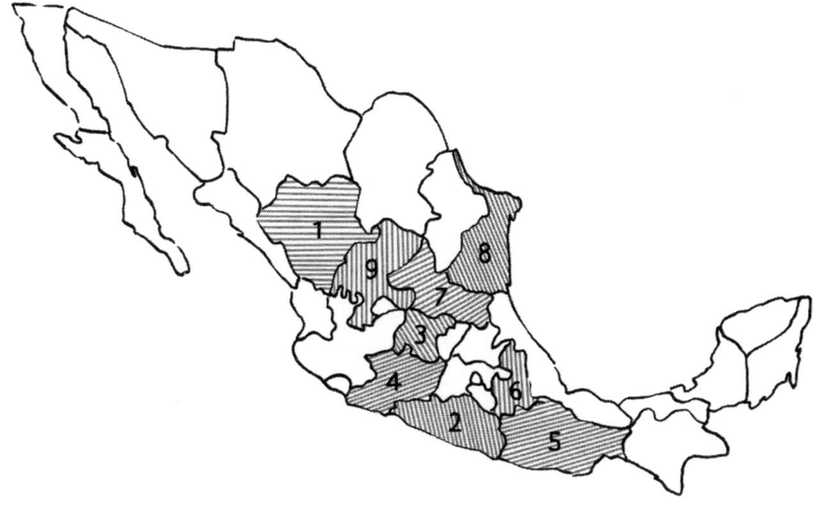

1 Durango
2 Guerrero
3 Guanajuato
4 Michoacán
5 Oaxaca
6 Puebla
7 San Luis Potosí
8 Tamaulipas
9 Zacatecas

Agaves

The human pursuit of making alcohol always starts out in the same place. We need to find a reliable, and preferably easy to work with, source of sugar. The source of sugar used varies wildly, depending on the climate and environment in which the producer resides. Scotland is damp and has a moody maritime climate, and as such it's pretty prime for growing barley. The midwestern United States is called the grain belt for a reason. In France, they do the grape thing. In the Caribbean the non-native sugar cane grows like a weed. For the entirety of human history, people have learned how to cultivate crops that can conveniently result in the production of booze, each according to where you are and what you've got.

Barely edging out Columbus, humans first came to the new world somewhere around 18,000 years ago. In the Americas, humans encountered a host of new resources and challenges: marshes and wetlands in the Midwestern United States, crazy intense mountains in the Andes, bone-dry desert in the American Southwest, and countless other extreme environmental conditions. In the South of Mexico, our early ancestors faced some unique challenges indeed. While not exactly a desert as we'd imagine it, the south of Mexico is on the whole extremely arid. The land can support corn cultivation, but in such a dry area it's a precious food source. People love to imbibe, but not when it means going hungry.

Humans are omnivores, and omnivores are weird. Autotrophic organisms, like plants, are able to create energy, harvesting nutrients like water and minerals in the process. Climbing the up the food chain, most organisms depend on the energy and nutrients created and harvested by these autotrophs. We have the machinery to create some of the things we need on our own, but others have to come from our diet. Certain nutrients are more elusive than others, and B vitamins are rather tricky for humans to obtain. The easiest way for us to obtain them is by eating animals. Mesoamericans didn't have steady access to animal protein.

Without having farm animals, they had to rely on hunting wild game as their only chance to occasionally have meat for dinner.

Through sheer ingenuity, Mesoamericans realized that by turning corn into masa, they could survive by eating mostly corn alone. What they didn't know was that the process of making masa frees up B vitamins in the corn and allows humans to digest them. Masa was immeasurably crucial as a staple of the proto-Mexican diet. Corn was essential to survival, and as such, it was simply too important to turn into booze.

The very conditions that posed a challenge to early humans did so for plant life as well. Us humans tend to use our big brains to adapt to our environment. Plants have no choice but to depend on the slow and steady forces of evolution to shape their form and function. When we think of plants fine-tuned to thrive in an arid environment, the first things that comes to mind are cactuses. There are a whole host of other plants that get on well in similar conditions, and arguably the most important to early Mesoamericans was the agave.

Agaves have spent millions of years slowly adapting to what would seem to us to be less-than-ideal environmental conditions. Like all desert plants, they are experts at obtaining and storing water. Once captured, they protect this water tenaciously. The ecological harshness agaves encountered formed them into many shapes and sizes, each sharing a host of specific genetic adaptations making them fit to live in one of the most challenging environments.

Agaves range greatly in size. On the small end, some reach only a foot or two tall, while other species can grow well over 10 feet in height. They all share the same basic layout, with leaves radiating out from a central mass of starch. They are incredibly hardy and can survive with very little water for long periods of time. The maturation and life cycle of agaves are significantly affected by both species and environment. Some can expect to live for as few as six years, while others may continue to grow for 30 years or more. To uncover a bit more detail about the inner workings of these rugged plants, we're going to need to look at the cause of their indefatigable tenacity: evolution.

Monocot

When it comes to 'modern' flowering plants, there are two main types: monocots and eudicots. This sounds deceptively simple, but the differences all start with whether the plant initially sends up one shoot out of its seed or two. Most monocots send up only one initial shoot, but there's a whole host of factors that set them apart from eudicots. The world of plants is vast, and there's a great deal of variation within these two groups too, but we can generalize that monocots trend towards having simpler growth patterns and less diverse structures. The leaves and flowers of eudicots are more complex than those of monocots, and as they grow, eudicots execute a more complicated plan. Most leaf-bearing trees are good examples of eudicots. They've got bark covering them, a trunk holding them up and housing a highly organized system of inter-plant transport, and leaves that are made of different stuff than the trunk.

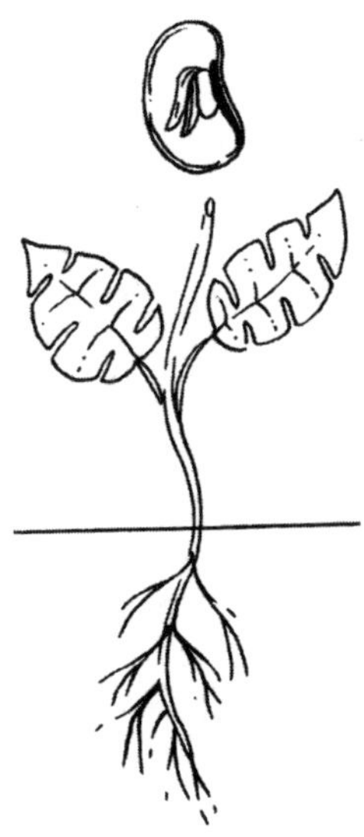

Eudicot

In the world of plants, as well as life in general, more complicated isn't necessarily better. Agaves are monocots, and as such the way they grow is incredibly iterative. What does that mean? Imagine you have to explain to someone how to draw a five-pointed star. Each step is the same as the last. Draw a short line, stop, change the angle by about 70 degrees, and draw a line of the same length. Do this four times and you have a form that's more complicated than the instructions you followed. This precise, albeit repetitive, process is how agaves grow. Agaves consist of little more than their leaves and their roots.

When agaves grow from seed, they initially shoot up their single cotiledon. Concurrently the business-end of the plant is developing in the opposite direction. The shoot clears a path upwards while the root grows equally down. A small slit opens in the side of the initial shoot and out of it emerges the beginnings of the plant's most characteristic structure: the rosette. The rosette is the primary structure of the agave and is where we see the iterative growth patterns that define this type of plant. At first, two leaves emerge together to form the rosette, one curled inside and opposed to the other. As the plant grows, other leaves appear one-by-one inside, each growing larger than the last. The inner growth pushes the outer leaves out, and the plant grows in size. Agaves continue this general growth pattern until their reproduction and death, which we'll speak about later.

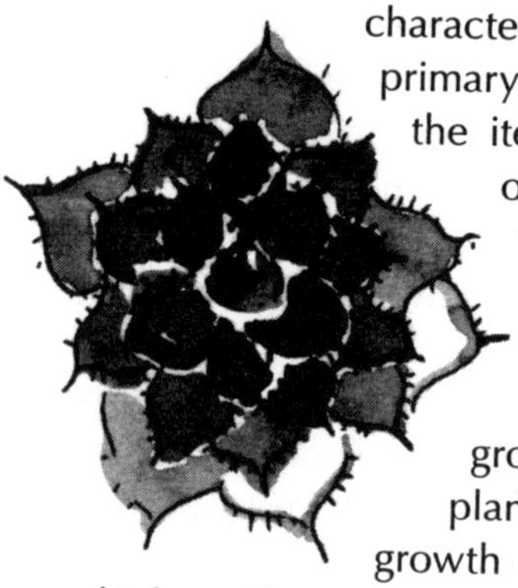

The leaves, also called *pencas,* and the roots are the only real structures that agaves have. The roots are shallow and quickly absorb any moisture in the soil. The rosette arrangement of the leaves conveniently routes any rainfall to the base of the plant, where it can be rapidly soaked up by the plant's shallow roots before it drains out of the soil. The leaves of the agave are where energy is both created and stored. As the plant grows, the area at the base of each leaf connects within the rosette to form the heart of the agave, or *piña* in mezcal parlance. The plant stores its energy in the piña in the form of those fructans we talked about earlier, which are of prime concern if our goal is to end up with mezcal.

As anyone who's had an unexpected encounter with a cactus can tell you, desert plants tend to lead with a strong defense. A plant growing out in the open on a relatively barren landscape containing life-giving water and thousands of calories of nutrients is a prime target for just about any creature that might find it. While the cactus favors defenses that are a bit more ostentatious, agaves go a more subtle route.

Most species of agaves produce chemical irritants, present on their surface and in their sap. The first time I went to Jalisco and visited an agave field I accidentally brushed up against an agave while walking past. The subsequent rash on my arm took months to go away. Many agave species have also evolved hooked spikes along the outside of their leaves and sharp, pointed tips for their pencas. Agaves in the fields and mountains of Mexico have established that they are not to be trifled with.

In the areas where agaves grow, water is a prized resource. Once obtained, it's something that plants and animals alike want to hold on to for as long as they can. Agaves are very good at operating with minimal water available, and one of the ways that they achieve that is by avoiding losing water whenever possible.

Typically, plants perform photosynthesis while they respirate—they make energy while they breathe. In this fashion, CO2 has to get into the plant, and it does so through pores on the plants surface. If a plant breathes while it makes energy, and it makes energy from the sun, it follows that the plant has to breathe while the sun is out. The sun beaming down on a plant means that some of that plant's water is going to come back out through those pores and evaporate in the heat of the day. For agaves, this just won't do. Agaves have evolved the ability to open their pores at night and store CO2 until the next day. They can then perform photosynthesis with their pores closed and thus lose minimal water. At night, the pores open back up and the oxygen produced from photosynthesis is released out into the air, and the cycle repeats. It turns out agaves are really good at holding their breath.

Agaves have evolved to deal well with stressful conditions. Rainy season in Oaxaca lasts only a few months. Outside of that, plants often go the whole year without receiving much in the way of water. In drought years, agaves can survive 12 or 18 months with minimal rainfall. Water stress can be seen physically in many species, with parts or all of their leaves taking on a bright red color.

Paradoxically, situations of extreme stress seem to often be of benefit for these rugged plants. Offsets seem to do best when replanted after intentional stressing. It's common for *palenqueros* to leave their offsets sitting in the sun for a month or two before planting them in the soil. The stressed condition of the plant makes it eager to root and seems to speed up the subsequent growth of the plant as well. Procrastinators among us can likely relate.

Agaves share the same goal as every other species on earth: reproduction. Agaves grow slowly and surely, saving energy their entire lives in hopes of flowering. How long it takes for an individual agave to reach sexual maturity is highly dependent on species and environment, but is generally from 8 to 15 years of age. When the time comes, the plant uses all its stored energy to shoot out an extremely phallic inflorescence. In mezcal parlance, this is called the *quiote*. This quiote grows like a giant stalk of asparagus out of the center of the rosette and generally rises to upwards of 30 feet tall, around three times taller than the plant itself. The quiote then produces flowers, either in a cone shape directly from the quiote itself, or from small branches that reach outward from the top. The plan is that bats and insects will pollinate these flowers and will eventually bear seed from which other agaves can grow. It's a fatalistic gesture predicated in extreme optimism, as producing the inflorescence consumes all the energy the plant has saved over its lifetime. Once the plant raises the stalk and forms the seeds, the agave promptly dies within weeks to a few months time.

One problem with reproduction from seed is germination time. Agaves grow relatively slowly. During rainy season there is an intense competition among plants to be the first to snatch up the precious water. Weeds specialize in a fast and furious lifecycle and often pose a considerable threat to agave propagation. Weeds grow dramatically quicker than the agave sprouts, thus denying the agaves access to sunlight and choking them out. For this reason, certain agave species tend to grow in odd places. Agave *potatorum*, also known as tobalá, has a habit of growing on the sides of cliffs. Tobalá seeds grow unusually slow and are quickly stifled by any competition. If the seeds fall onto the surface of a craggy cliff, competition is scarce, and the baby tobalá has a much better chance of making it.

Planning years ahead in an arid environment is a precarious proposition. Three consecutive years of drought can result in a dead agave and no second generation. As such, agaves have developed two other methods of reproduction by which to propagate their various species. In hedging against an untimely death, many agaves create structures called offsets, also known as *hijuelos*. An offset is a small clone produced by the agave near its base. The clone grows up from the roots of the mother plant and sets up shop. If the mother dies without finding other means to reproduce successfully, the offset carries on where the mother left off, in almost the same place as its forebearer. Agaves only produce offsets from their young-adult stage onwards, starting around three or four years into their lives. The number of offsets generated by an agave varies wildly by species, from producing none to producing a dozen or more over a lifetime. A significant disadvantage of offsets is their lack of genetic diversity—they are a genetic copy of the mother plant. A major advantage is that they can grow quickly using the resource of the mother plant, thus avoiding any threats of competition.

Another threat is lack of fertilization. What if the agave makes it all the way to flowering and doesn't get pollinated? Growing a quiote and flowering is a highly fatalistic act. The death of the plant prevents any subsequent attempts at reproduction. This means its multi-year effort was all for naught. Some agaves have developed a third method of reproduction in addition to flowering and the creation of offsets, the ability to produce bulbils. A bulbil is similar to an offset in that it is a genetic clone of the mother plant, but these offsets grow from the flowers on the quiote instead of seeds. Similar to offsets, bulbils can use the resource of the mother plant to get a head start. Unlike regular offsets, which seek to grow in the same territory as the mother plant, bulbils aim to break away from the quiote and attempt to root wherever they happen to land. Bulbil production varies widely by species. Some species rarely if ever produce them, while others produce them somewhat consistently.

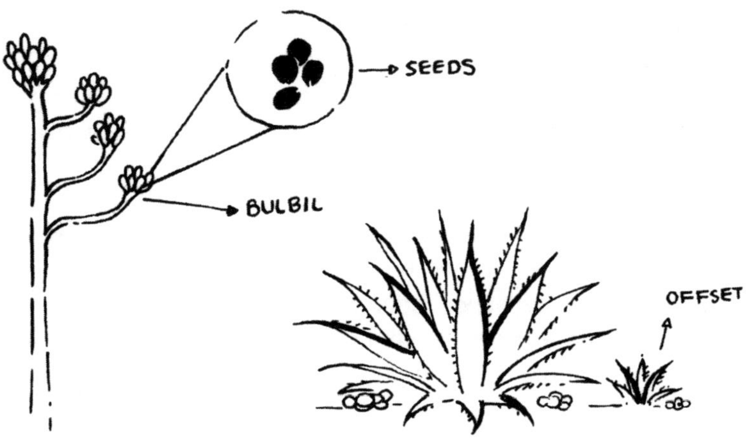

Agaves naturally range from the southern United States down to Central and South America. The location of maximum biodiversity is in the southern Mexican state of Oaxaca. The reason is twofold: it is likely the locus of origin in which agaves first evolved, and Oaxaca is also home to an incredible diversity of environments. Each of these environments placed different selective pressures on the plants and over time different species emerged.

All agaves around the world emanated from Mexico. They were transported across the globe for ornamental purposes and spread back to the wild. You can find them most places on Earth, ranging from Italy to Australia, where the temperature is warm enough. Agaves are even found in climates that have way more rainfall than they should have, as long as the plants grow in places that offer sufficient drainage.

Agaves are hardy, stubborn, and resilient plants. All of the evolutionary forces that shaped these traits had a very positive side effect: growing in such a harsh environment caused agaves to evolve the ability to produce a ton of chemicals that happen to create aroma and flavor. Seeing as our overall goal here is to end up drinking delicious spirits, we're off to a very good start.

These plants have been hard-wired by evolution to protect themselves and find any way possible to give life to the next generation. A deeper understanding of their unique biology has resulted in an ever-growing body of knowledge about how to propagate, maintain, and harvest these plants for human use. In the next chapter we will explore more deeply how humans and agaves interact, and the types of plants we humans tend to find the most useful.

Agaves & Humans

Agaves have been shaped to survive in their environment by the slow forces of evolution. Like all plants from arid climates, they've evolved unique solutions and have found ways to survive in places where others can't. It is in the evolution department that we humans are unique among all life on earth. It is true that living for tens of thousands of years in a specific environment can slowly begin to shape us physically. Take Northern Europeans and their freakish lack of melanin. Dark skin has a whole host of advantages. Not, however, when it comes to our bodies ability to produce vitamin D in low-sunlight environments. Examples where evolutionary forces shape humans who live in different environments are as numerous as they are generally subtle. When it comes to humans adapting to new environments, our big brains do the real heavy lifting.

Humans are unique in our ability to move into, adapt to, and thrive in almost any environment on the planet. When we migrate to a new place we take matters into our own hands. There may be no clearer example of this than native American housing types. From the Inuit and First Nations peoples all the way down the Tierra del Fuego at the southern tip of Chile, the same original settlers came to the Americas from Asia and spread out far and wide. Starting from the top, imagine igloos in the north, subterranean earthen lodges in the Dakotas, Tepees on the central plains, Pueblos in the South West, and airy, thatch-roofed huts in the Yucatán. Each dwelling is ideally suited for the environment the inhabitant faces: freezing cold, extreme temperature swings, chasing after herds of animals, arid and dry, or putting up with unbearable heat and humidity. We humans tend to do the changing while evolution lumbers behind.

Our ability to change our behavior and adapt to new environments is particularly useful when it comes to finding steady sources of food. The development of agriculture was a sure sign that we were thinking about the future. Sure, I can eat now, but I definitely want to guarantee that I can eat tomorrow as well. Each crop that we have collectively mastered has its preferred conditions, and it's up to us to use our big brains to make sure we're growing the best thing in the right place.

If you were an enterprising Mesoamerican, perhaps you would have noticed agaves thriving where no other plants could. Who knows how humans first learned the real potential of these plants? Legend has it that a well-aimed lightning strike did double duty in illustrating the usefulness of the agave as a crop. The bolt allegedly split an agave in half and effectively roasted the inside. The sweetness of the result would have been unmistakable to any hunter/gatherer as their dietary holy grail: sugar. Pure, raw energy.

The tricky part about these plants is the type of sugars that they make. Agaves produce simple fructose, which we know as the most common type of sugar found in fruit. They protect this fructose by binding multiple molecules together into chains called fructans. Fructans are unusable to animals as a source of energy—if we consume enough of them, we will die from chronic diarrhea. Our bodies just aren't equipped to break them down. For agaves, they provide a convenient means of energy storage that has the added benefit of making their sugars harder for other creatures to use.

Regardless of how the value of agaves was discovered, Mesoamericans wasted no time in learning how to live with and use these plants. The thorns could be used as needles, the fibers as string, and most importantly the piña could be cooked for food or its juices could be extracted and fermented. Going the fermentation route with agave is somewhat similar to the process of making maple syrup, a producer partially cuts and irritates the agave. In an attempt to heal itself, the plant rapidly begins turning the fructans back into sugar and releases them in the form of sap. This sap is collected and allowed to ferment naturally. The result is called *pulque,* which is a mild beer-like beverage with around 4-8% alcohol volume. It's important to note that some types of agaves are better for this than others, and the ones that serve well for pulque production tend to be rather large.

We know that by the mid-1600s distillates were being made from agave and that they were an important part of both provincial and urban life in Mexico. Distilled spirits from agave appear in legal and regulatory documents and travelers at the time reference *vino de mezcal* and its intoxicating powers. The cultural impact of mezcal was now self-evident, but how long had agave spirits been a part of Mexican life?

That's where things get a bit speculative. We know for a fact that the Mesoamericans made pulque. Clay fragments have been found with the residue of fermented agave sap on them. We also know that they cut agaves, roasted their piñas, and used them for food. What remains unknown is whether or not they developed the technology to concentrate the low-alcohol fermented agave into a high-concentration spirit before the Spaniards came to North America. The most provocative element of this equation, and the missing link between pulque and spirit, lies in plain sight: the still. A still is the piece of equipment needed to separate alcohol from water with the intent of concentrating the one by eliminating much of the other. Modern-day mezcal is produced using two distinctly different types of stills. The first is a European-style copper still, and the other is a very rustic Filipino-style clay pot still.

Here's the thing: for me, pre-Hispanic distillation is like the X-Files. I want to believe. I really, really do. Some folks speculate that perhaps Mesoamericans had contact with Asia and the technology migrated across the Pacific Ocean. Unfortunately, the contact-with-the-east thing seems pretty unlikely. The Bering Land Bridge appears to have disappeared about 11,000 years ago, significantly predating early Chinese distillation. If anybody went back and forth, they didn't walk. Alternative contact routes with the east also seem improbable, and if they did exist, we would definitely expect to see a greater broad cultural impact from this contact, not just one piece of technology.

This leaves us with the lone possibility of the self-discovery of distillation by Mesoamerican peoples. While there is no way to present evidence that this didn't happen, no one has yet to discover conclusive evidence that it did. These points have forced me to currently take the personal stance that pre-Columbian distillation did not happen in Mexico. I would very much love to be proved wrong on this subject, as it would be a testament to the ingenuity and cultural sophistication of the Mesoamerican peoples. One single conclusive discovery could dispel any doubt, but it would take a bit more than that to prove that distillation had broader cultural importance in pre-Columbian Mexico. If distillation were going on back then, it would have been a huge deal.

There is still a lively, active debate surrounding this issue. Beliefs about pre-Columbian distillation have a real legal impact on which mezcales are deemed to come from 'ancestral' traditions. Aside from this issue lies the reality: palenqueros have used both copper and clay stills for hundreds of years. Both are extremely important traditions that result in incredible products. We're dedicating an entire chapter to distillation, so we'll have plenty of time to talk about differences produced by the two types of stills and other variants seen throughout Mexico.

Up until the last few hundred years humans viewed agave a bit more like fresh water and a bit less like corn. Corn has been subject to cultivation and planting for thousands of years. To have corn reliably at our disposal, we must grow it ourselves. Water, however, is a resource that is found, not cultivated. We establish our sources of water, and if they run dry or become foul, we go and find new ones. For a long time, humans mostly made use of the agaves that happened to grow around them. There was an abundant supply, and each agave was already growing in an environment in which it thrived. This began to change as the mezcal tradition in Jalisco began to slowly morph into the category that we know today as Tequila. Like all things surrounding tequila production, cultivation enterprisingly focused on economic viability. The more sugar a plant produces, the more alcohol it will yield.

Before we go any farther, we need to talk a bit about taxonomy. One of the most confusing things about mezcal is the preponderance of agave types, which we'll explore momentarily. Mezcal being a highly regional spirit has resulted in a vast body of terminology used to describe the diversity of agaves employed in its production. Vexingly, these local bodies of knowledge have vast areas of overlap, resulting in things being called different names in different regions. My first instinct is to turn to the realm of science to attempt to tether these local names and descriptions to something more concrete.

This is where things start to get really tricky. The scientific system of taxonomy begins with the universal ancestor of all life on earth and narrows down into smaller and smaller groups based less on shared traits and more on common ancestors. Each category has specific criterion and allows us to tell with relative ease how closely related any two species are in the tree of life. At its narrowest end, we have organisms grouped together, each into their own close-knit genus and finally into their respective species. The definition of a species is deceptively simple: any two members of the same species should be able to reproduce, and their offspring must be able to have more offspring. Donkeys and horses aren't the same species because despite being able to interbreed, mules are always born sterile. This all seems very sensible but gets drastically more complicated in species containing a significant amount of genetic diversity.

All human beings are the same genus and species, *Homo sapiens*. All dogs are as well, *Canis familiaris*. A Great Dane and a Chihuahua are the same species, and despite some serious logistical hurdles, they can produce viable offspring. The reason we have so many names for different breeds of dogs is reflective of a need to describe their variations. What makes them different? How big are they? What do they look like? What can we do with them? We face these same challenges of description when we look at agave types as well. Just because they are the same species doesn't account for the differences in the genetics among plants or how their environment will shape their usefulness.

Agaves are also notoriously difficult to describe scientifically. What initially appear to be two entirely different species are sometimes the exact same. Scientists are always actively working on making sure that species are described correctly and are placed in the right bigger groups. We have to acknowledge that when we're using taxonomy as our guide, we will always be standing on moving ground. Not too long ago agaves were moved from the subfamily *Lilliales* to the subfamily *Asparagales*. This in no way means that agaves aren't related to lilies, but rather that the path of their evolution from common ancestors was just a little different than we thought it was.

When we learn about agaves, we need to take into account not only genus and species but also local name. There's often a bit of triangulating between both, and the uncertainty surrounding these plants will still be alive and well when I'm very much not. These are important things to know and understand but are by no means worthy of bogging us down.

One particularly interesting case-study in naming and politics surrounds the type of agave used to make tequila. The aptly-named

Agave tequilana Weber v. azul, also known as Weber blue agave, is the only type of agave the CRT permits for the production of tequila. It is a type of agave that grows quickly, generally reaching maturity in 7 to 10 years. It also produces a large amount of sugar which makes it a natural choice for using to make spirits. This particular agave began widespread cultivation in the early 1800s. It is understood to be a close relative of *Agave angustifolia,* commonly known in the mezcal world as *espadín. Agave tequiliana* is a name which is incredibly on-brand, and it should come as no surprise that tequila producers had a heavy hand in its naming and description as a species. There is one small problem, in that *A. tequilana Weber* and *A. angustifolia* can not only interbreed but also produce viable offspring when they do. Our elementary definition of species tells us that this means they're one in the same. As a subtle act of protest, this book treats them as the same species. Sorry tequileros, it makes me very unhappy when you mess with my science.

Before we get down into specifics, a few things about agave cultivation in general. One persistent source of confusion surrounds differences between 'cultivated' and 'wild' species. Popular dogma and much brand education surrounds a big distinction between agaves that are planted and grown by humans and agaves that are allegedly unplantable. Let's make a case study of Oaxaca 2018. Currently, the only significant type of cultivated agave being used to produce mezcal in Oaxaca is Agave espadín. Effectively all the other expressions known to consumers—*tobalá, tepextate,* all the *karwinskii*s, etc.—are being wild harvested.

Let's take a step back and define this. We'll define cultivation as humans planting agave from seed, bulbil, or offset. We'll also define it

as humans planting those agaves in a group or field in some organized way. When driving through Oaxaca, rows of planted espadín are visible in valleys and on hillsides. We'll also define wild as seeds or offsets which have spontaneously ended up taking root and growing without human intervention. Driving into the foothills of the Sierra Norte of Oaxaca, one can see dozens upon dozens of *Agave potatorum* growing out of the sides of the surrounding cliffs. Ostensibly nobody planted them there, only Mother Nature herself.

Any human relationship with a naturally occurring resource must either exist in balance or eventually suffer the consequences. Something tells me that in the year 2100 we're not going to be pulling oil out of the ground. Unlike oil, agaves are reproducing themselves. The question is, are they reproducing fast enough to replenish what we humans are harvesting? One of the biggest impediments to sufficient wild propagation is the means by which agaves reproduce. In a few chapters, you'll see a list of agaves types and notes on their preferred methods of reproduction.

If an agave type primarily propagates via seed, the mother plant must live out its whole life cycle and produce a quiote with flowers that a bat or insect will hopefully pollinate. The problem with this is that after the agave produces a quiote, the plant is useless for making mezcal. The plant uses up all the energy it has saved over its life and dies. One option is to cut off the growing quiote, stifling its growth. The confused plant halts the use of its sugars to grow its quiote and instead re-concentrates them in the heart of the plant. After a month or two, the piña can once again be used to make mezcal, but the plant never got the chance to flower and go to seed. This process, called *capón,* which translates to English as castration, shuts down the plant's last efforts to make offspring.

Because the economic needs of mezcal producers are fundamentally antithetical, producers harvest a majority of sought-after agaves before they're able to blossom and reproduce. Wild harvesting in this way drastically favors types of agaves that propagate by offset, thus changing the natural distribution of agave types and determining which agaves will be more readily available in the future. Because bulbil reproduction also requires the growth of the quiote, plant types that prefer this method of reproduction are also at a distinct disadvantage.

Upon first reading, this is an extremely alarming situation. No matter the future of mezcal, the naturally occurring ecosystem of these plants hangs in the balance. Our further discussion is in no way trying to diminish the serious nature of this potential environmental crisis. Naturally existing ecosystems are simultaneously robust and delicate, and human interaction has the real potential to screw things up. There are, however, a few other things to consider when thinking on this subject.

One extremely positive benefit of this situation for the mezcal business is the perceived scarcity of these so-called wild types of agave. If I try to sell you a bottle of wine recovered from the Titanic, the price is going to be astronomical. If you discover that a total of 200,000 bottles were salvaged from the depths, the price is going to take a drastic nose-dive. The idea of rarity plays a key role in the pricing of mezcales made from other types of agave. Most consumers of mezcal are extremely removed from the actual economics of production. We are often forced to rely on second or third-hand information about the current market and environmental conditions. This is a highly advantageous situation for those creating the pricing, and it also incentivizes the perpetuation of certain myths and stereotypes surrounding agaves and their cultivation.

Economics can be a beautiful thing. The power of the market is so often the driving force of innovation. When there is money to be made, people have a knack for creating a path towards a more sustainable future. All over Oaxaca folks are working on ways to grow and domesticate all the types of agave from which they make mezcal. Some varieties are more finicky than others, but these are hearty plants determined to grow. These are no delicate orchids or shrinking violets. Despite having preferred conditions for growth, agaves are persistent plants and have broad environmental adaptability.

The widespread efforts to understand cultivation of various agave types are finding success. Greenhouses have sprung up in multiple towns and the first transplantings of agave tobalá and tepextate, which usually prefer more exotic and far-flung environs, are just now beginning to come of age. I've seen tobalá in the form of seedlings in Santiago Matatlán in a palenquero's garden, a nursery for young plants in Santa Catarina Minas, a mix of young and maturing plants in Candelaria Yegolé, and 300 standing 8-year-old tobalá planted in neat rows, deep in the Sierra Norte. All over Oaxaca, these efforts are coming to fruition. In the foreseeable future, there will be a slow shift away from environmental depletion towards self-sustained growing efforts of these sought-after plants.

The economic influences that are causing innovation also have a considerable downside. Capitalism rewards the innovative and the lazy alike. As long as mature wild plants are growing, and as long as they have a financial value to humans, there will be incentive to over-harvest. No matter how forward-thinking or self-sufficient agave growing efforts become, the temptation of reaping the benefits of 12 years of nature's hard work in an instant will be too provocative for some to resist. This presents a problem that can only be adequately addressed through the means of law and regulation. Agaves are hardy plants, but no level of fortitude can overcome the machinations of humans in search of an easy paycheck.

As we move towards greater agave cultivation efforts, there are those who preemptively lament the loss of the unique terroir obtained by making mezcal from wild-grown agave. In my mind, there is no doubt that there will be differences between wild-harvested and estate-grown, especially as we humans first begin to try to understand these complicated plants. Growers must pay much attention to making sure that each type of plant grows in its preferred environment and that each plant is given the best approximation of its natural conditions possible. Regardless, the recent developments in agave agriculture run counter to much of the information perpetuated by those with interest in making money from selling mezcal. I, for one, find great hope in the move towards humans working more closely with and understanding these plants. It's the continuation of a longstanding relationship, in which the agave has given life and sustenance to the people of Mexico for thousands of years and portends to do so into the future.

Making Mezcal

We now have a strong understanding of agaves as plants and the basics of how they fit into the lives of those who produce mezcal. The time has come for us to look under the hood and start to understand the layers of intricacy that make mezcal a universe unto itself.

We already investigated how agaves store energy. The fructans that agaves produce are a tactical choice—they bind the sugars into forms unusable by us pesky humans and other interested actors. The beauty of this arrangement is that those fructans are relatively easy to unlock. Just apply heat. Mesoamerican peoples learned how to cook agave and use it as food. The only problem with cooking is that it takes some time and technique. Just like cooking a roast or beef short rib, low and slow is the key to getting fructans to break down into simple fructose.

In our modern world when we want to cook something low and slow, we just pop it in the oven and set the temperature. Agave piñas tend to be large, and generally, when producing mezcal, we'd like to roast more than one at a time. Ideally, we'd also like to use as little fuel as possible - in this case, firewood. The solution is brilliantly simple. Mesoamericans learned to dig shallow pits and turn the earth into an oven. Soil is an excellent insulator and is also very free. These methods persist today in the work of agave spirits producers all over Mexico. Workers at the palenque generally fill a pit with firewood which is allowed to cook down into charcoal. The palenqueros then cover the charcoal with rocks and when the time is right, whole or cut agave piñas. The piñas are stacked and cut in a way as to ensure even cooking. The piñas are then generally covered—often with spent agave fibers, tarps, cloth, damp straw mats, or anything else—and the palenquero covers them with dirt for insulation. The average roast for making mezcal is around five days, including time to load and unload the earthen oven.

As is the case with all things tequila, modernity, and industrialization prevailed. More rustic tequila producers employ large brick ovens powered by steam. Cooking time with a brick oven is generally around 36 hours. The more progress-minded tequila producers make use of large autoclaves. Autoclaves are effectively large pressure cookers, which can allow the cooking time to be cut as low as 12 hours. Producers in search of ultimate efficiency use machines called diffusers. While capable of extracting up to 99.9% of agave sugars, all kinds of nasty tricks need to be employed to get these beasts to work right. Diffusers effectively strip agave fibers of their fructan chains without cooking them, and they do this by using high-pressure water sprayers and chemicals. Additives abound, notoriously including sulphuric acid. After producers remove the juice, it must be cooked, which is expeditiously performed in autoclaves in liquid form, rather than roasting the agave piñas whole. For reasons shrouded in secrecy, fermentations of juice produced by diffusers tend to stall, resulting in producers using additives as fermentation accelerants.

After roasting, the agaves must be milled. The sugars we want remain trapped in between incredibly tough fibers, and crushing them is the easiest way to get them out. The most ancient way of accomplishing this is by placing the agave piñas in wooden troughs or stone pits and mashing them by hand with large wooden mallets. I cannot emphasize this enough, milling by hand is possibly the single most strenuous work a human being can perform. It takes its toll on the whole body. Feet, hands, arms, back, neck: arduous repetitive motion attacks the body. Delicate humans such as I do well to withstand a few minutes at this task, let alone multiple eight-hour days per week. The implementation of this technique varies by region, sometimes employing giant wooden bats or machetes, but the level of effort required stays relatively constant. A good handful of small producers still go to the length of hand milling, as it's often the technique that's been passed to them from generations before.

One step towards modernity arrived in the introduction of the *tahona.* The tahona is a giant stone wheel, often made out of a single volcanic stone or made out of smaller stones and concrete. A horse or donkey usually roll the tahona around a circular stone-lined pit in which the stone crushes the agave piñas. This is often tough work for both man and animal, as the palenquero must mush the animal around the circular pit for hours a day and move the agave fibers about. Some palenqueros have switched out the animal for motorized means of pulling the tahona. Another method used is mechanical mills. Small milling machines that resemble wood chippers are common, and larger roller mills which spray the fibers with water to aid in extraction are also an option. Tequila producers widely use the large roller mills, while the smaller shredders more frequently find use in mezcal country.

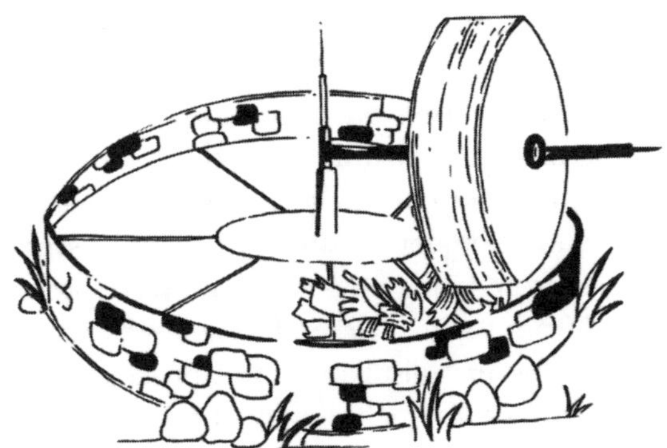

Let me take a moment to opine: I am against the use of any gasoline-powered machines around or near the production of mezcal. Several years ago the Mexican government took it upon themselves to purchase simple and portable shredding machines on behalf of many producers. The problem with these is they're all gasoline powered.

Imagine a small wood-chipper on wheels. The decision makes a degree of sense, as some of the areas where producers will use the machines don't have consistent access to electrical power. The biggest flub is that the machines the producers received emphasized portability when the reality is that each one will likely always be used in just one place. We live in a world where we have no choice but to breathe in fumes every day. I prefer taking precaution to keep these out of our food and drink wherever possible. For every application of gasoline near production at a *palenque,* there are other potential solutions that *palenqueros* could use instead. At the least, we should take efforts to separate the activities of burning fossil fuel and producing beverage alcohol.

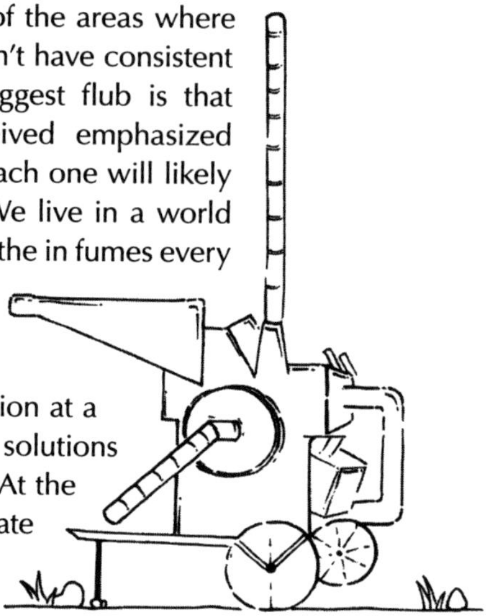

Regardless of the method of cooking or milling, making spirits from agave inherently requires dealing with the plant's fibers. The fibers don't make it into the bottle, and thus have to be separated out at some point in the production process. Most tequila producers separate out and dispose of the fibers before fermentation. Mezcal is unique in that most of the time these fibers make their way into fermentation, and often into the first distillation as well. Agave fibers are chemically complex. They contain oils and waxes that are slowly extracted into the fermenting liquid and add to the rich body and complex flavor of mezcal. Keeping these fibers around precludes many elements of streamlining or modernization. They prevent palenqueros from being able to use pumps, forcing the crushed agave to be moved from the mill to the fermenter by hand. If producers include the fibers in the first distillation, this process must be repeated once more to load in the stills. Including the fibers in the still also means more of a mess to clean up after the first distillation is complete. Making mezcal is by nature a very hands-on process, and the extra work involved pays dividends in the results.

After milling, palenqueros load the sugary-sweet runoff of the crushed agave (and usually the fibers as well) into a large fermenting tank. These tanks, or *tinas,* generally range in size between 500 and

1,200 liters. Commonly these are made of wood, though palenqueros use a great many other containers as well. It's worthy to note that as a palenquero increases the production capacity of his palenque, adding more tinas is almost always the preferred solution. The modular nature of growing one's operation one tina or one small still at a time enables small producers to grow within their means. Depending on the location, palenqueros also use leather cow hides, holes dug in rocks, concrete, plastic, and all manner of materials to contain the fermentation. In tequila country, 10,000-liter stainless steel tanks are common. After the agave juice and potentially the fibers find their way inside the fermenter of choice, water is added to dissolve the sugars and to dilute them. Sugar is food for yeast, but at high concentrations it's anti-microbial and prevents fermentation from happening. Once the agave sugars are diluted with water, the magic of fermentation can begin.

All alcoholic beverages are the result of fermentation. In its simplest form, fermentation is the process in which brewer's yeast grows in a liquid, eats sugar to produce energy, and creates alcohol and CO2 as a byproduct. In the production of most alcoholic beverages, this is an extremely controlled process. As a case study, let's consider beer. Anyone who has ever brewed beer can tell you that 90% of time spent brewing is, in reality, cleaning and sanitizing everything used in the process. The proto-beer is boiled and then cooled, placed in a sterile container, and finally, a specific strain of yeast is added to begin fermentation. That particular strain of yeast is always a member of the same genus and species: *Saccharomyces cerevisiae*. The goal is to make alcohol, but in practice, yeast does more than just that. Yeast is a living organism, and its reproduction, its death, and its production of alcohol all involve creating and breaking down a whole host of different chemicals. Despite its best efforts, yeast always leaves behind various amounts of these chemicals, creating distinctive flavors. Brewing enthusiasts have selected and cultivated different strains of yeast over time to produce a broad range of flavors and aromas. This one little bug has been so crucial to the flavor and consistency of beer that it has driven some of the most established brewers to go to great lengths to protect their proprietary yeasts from outsiders.

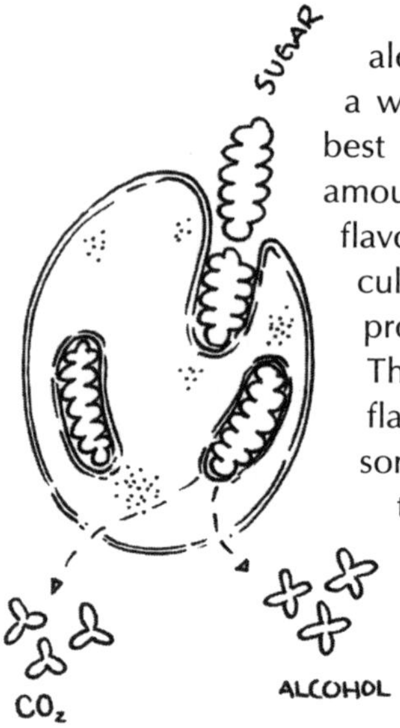

While not nearly as ostensible, this same chicanery goes on with spirits. Scotch whiskey producers speak in hushed tones about their proprietary yeast strains, guarded in the safety of the distillery's laboratory. Yeast is one of the ineffable factors that give most spirits their character. Delicate and controlled fermentation is one of the most crucial steps in making a spirit that is delicious and consistent. This is where mezcal production jumps entirely off the rails.

Brewers and distillers have been working with yeast for far longer than they've known exactly what yeast was. People have likely been making and drinking beer as long as they've been cultivating grain. For reference, that was probably round about 15,000 years ago. Louis Pasteur didn't discover yeast until 1857, which is comparatively pretty late in the game. Before pristine laboratories and sanitary conditions, brewers and distillers had only two options: try to preserve yeast from a previous batch or let nature run its course.

Yeast is all around us. Individual yeast cells are floating around you right now, whether you're outside in a park or crammed inside of a fully booked flight. Yeast cells, much like human beings, are opportunists. Like a seed hoping to be scattered and land in a favorable location to grow, yeast looks for an opportunity to come into contact with sugar. It grows on the skins of fruits, patiently waiting for those fruits to fall and rot. It's pretty much everywhere. This was a massive stroke of luck for early brewers. Take some grain, malt it, boil it in water, and leave the resulting liquid outside. A few days later this liquid started to bubble, almost magically. A few days after that, what was once sweet is now dry and slightly tart. Invite the friends and neighbors over; there's beer to be drunk.

Bonus points for efficacy, but this early beer had a few problems. One of the biggest was consistency. Some batches would have come out simpler and more similar to the beer we drink today. Some would taste very tart, sometimes like vinegar. Some would have odd, off flavors and aromas - mousey, horsey, barnyard flavors. In allowing our beer to come into contact with the outside world, we let in not only the yeast we want but also a bunch of other microbial critters that we don't. When it comes to floating microbes, yeast isn't the only game in town. A whole host of single-cell organisms fall into the beer and start to do their business. *Lactobacillus, Acetobacter, Brettanomyces,* and many many more.

Anybody who would actively choose to give up control and risk ruining their fermentation must be crazy. Those among us who enjoy sour beers can attest that sometimes being a bit crazy has its rewards. When experienced hands combine with a bit of luck and consistency of practice, amazing things can result. The flavors of grain and hops almost entirely comprise the flavors of regular beer, while its controlled yeast strain provides a subtle supporting role. An expertly made wild fermented sour beer speaks to a whole host of crazy flavors. Most readily apparent, it is bracingly tart. It's herbaceous, funky, toasty, and dry. We've taken a typical beer and added layer after layer of flavor on top, ending up with something way different than what we started with, but still speaking to the flavors of the grains which we used.

Quality mezcal is always wild fermented, and this style of fermentation takes time. When a brewer pitches yeast into beer, alcoholic fermentation is usually fully finished in around three days. In this situation the yeast has been given a head start, having been allowed to reproduce and become healthy before coming into contact with the sugary liquid. True spontaneous fermentation takes a bit more time to get started, as the yeast and other microbes that land in the fermenter have to reproduce and get ready to do their jobs, resulting in a longer minimum fermentation time than in a more clinical setting.

A 5-day wild fermentation results in a simpler mezcal abundant with flavors of slow-cooked agave. Middle-of-the-road fermentation time is somewhere between six and eight days. The level of acidity will be notably more pronounced, and the wild yeast will have a more significant impact on flavor. A 12- to 15-day fermentation is at the high end of the typical range, though some producers ferment for 30 days or longer. Longer fermentation time is not qualitatively better; it's just different. Several factors including ambient temperature affect the length of the fermentation time as well. If it's hotter out, the wild yeast do their business faster. If it's too cold, they may slow to a stop or never get started to begin with. Decisions made by a palenquero related to fermentation have some of the biggest impacts on how a given mezcal will taste.

One of the most significant factors determining the path a fermentation will take is access to oxygen. *Saccharomyces cerevisiae* does what we want it to do, make alcohol, only in anaerobic conditions—in an environment without oxygen. Just like us, yeast can create energy with or without oxygen. For us humans, one option is drastically better than the other. When we have oxygen, we produce energy with little more than CO2 as a byproduct. When oxygen is in short supply, our bodies switch to generate energy through anaerobic means, and that results in the production of lactic acid. You know this as the nasty cramps you get when exerting yourself too hard. For yeast, anaerobic is what we're after, as it's not only yeast's preferred way to make energy but the only way it will produce alcohol.

Water inherently has oxygen dissolved in it. When yeast encounters a cozy location to set up shop—say, a giant tank filled with roasted agave and water—it begins to replicate itself. Yeasts start wildly reproducing, preparing to do what they do best. This reproduction period is called the lag phase of fermentation, and it requires that the yeast have access to oxygen. By the time the yeast are done reproducing and are ready to get down to business, most of the oxygen in the environment is used up. This newfound anaerobic environment is perfect for yeast to begin consuming sugar in earnest and creating alcohol.

Certain bacteria and yeast prefer an anaerobic environment while others prefer an aerobic environment. Additionally, these critters operate in different ways and produce different aromas and flavors depending on whether they have access to oxygen or not. Palenqueros can introduce oxygen into the mix by simply pushing down the agave fibers that have formed a cap at the top of the fermenter. Use of this technique varies palenquero to palenquero, and ultimately has a surprising impact on the end result. Another common technique is adding water to the fermenting liquid. This serves to not only further dilute the concentration of sugar but also to lower the temperature of the fermentation, effectively pumping the brakes on the whole process.

The ambient temperature at the palenque is firmly outside the palenqueros control. If they're located high in the mountains or down by the coast, they may experience extreme temperatures that are outside the comfort zone of *Saccharomyces cerevisiae*. Brewer's yeast has a very narrow temperature range in which it can operate effectively: around 65-75 degrees Fahrenheit. Outside this window, the brewer's yeast's activity slows down drastically, allowing other microbes to thrive and snatch up more real estate inside the fermenter. Because of this, we see a surprising similarity in results from both low ambient temperature and high ambient temperature fermentations: a lot more funky flavors and aromas.

On to the last step of the journey, distillation. Everything boils at a different temperature. Water boils at 212° Fahrenheit and ethanol, our intoxicating friend, boils at 173°. When we heat up a liquid, the various chemicals in it start to break away and float through the still. The lighter these chemicals are, the easier it is for them to do so. This simple truth is the cornerstone behind the idea of distilled spirits, and we'll talk about it in painstaking detail a bit later on. If we're really slick and relatively careful, we can take a low-alcohol fermented beverage and concentrate it down into something much more potent.

To do this, we need a still, which we already discussed briefly in the preceding chapter. A still is effectively a sealed pot in which a liquid boils. In a copper alembic still, the vapors rise through a copper

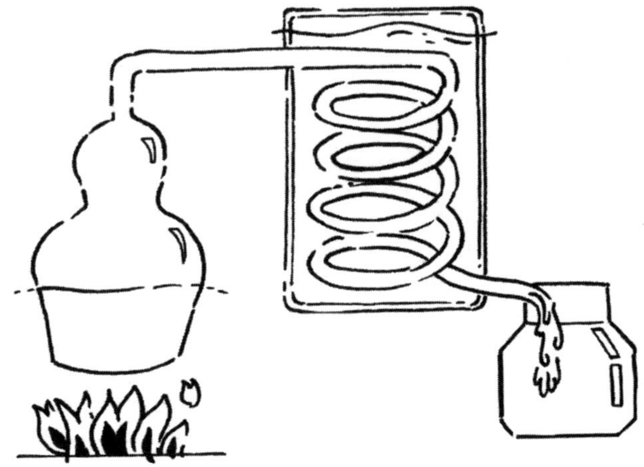

Cooper Alembic Still

tube called a swan's neck and into a coils running through cold water to condense it. A clay pot still circumvents all that. A clay still is generally comprised of two clay pots sealed together and topped with a metal pan holding cold water. An agave leaf or other collector sits under the metal pan and collects drops of condensed mezcal. These drops run down a bamboo-like tube and are collected outside the still. Copper pot stills in Oaxaca tend to be of simple design and relatively uniform. Clay pot stills are handmade and tend to have a bit more variation. Numerous variants on both types are scattered all throughout Mexico. In the Western mountains of Oaxaca and on into central Mexico, hollowed out tree trunks, combinations of copper and clay, and repurposed stainless steel cooking vessels are all crafted into ingenious devices used to make spirits.

Clay Pot Still

When speaking about distillation, where the palenquero cuts the distillate is one of the most concerning points. Heads, which boil away first, usually contain alcohols other than ethanol that are harmful to human beings in concentration. Tails are what we take off at the end of the distillation, and they contain off and bitter flavors, a lot of water, and very little alcohol. Using agave as a source material has one very unintended consequence that changes the calculus behind how mezcal and tequila are cut. When distilling spirits, one of our main enemies is methanol. Methanol is the stuff that makes you go blind if you drink too much of it, or have a really gnarly hangover if you drink slightly less. Methanol has a boiling point of 148.5° F. Using what we know about distillation, it boils at a lower temperature and should be one of the first things to go up and through our still. In the production of almost all other spirits, it is. With mezcal, this is where things get a bit... complicated.

Some compounds have an attraction to others. Ethanol loves water so much that it's almost impossible to separate the two entirely. Even if a distiller were able to isolate 100% pure ethanol, ethanol would wick water out of the atmosphere until the mixture contained about 3% water by volume. Attractive relationships like these can get stronger or weaker depending on the concentration of one compound to the other. At a certain point, called an azeotrope, their attraction is at its maximum, and the two liquids stick together like glue. This process changes their boiling point. For reasons well outside the scope of this book, depending on the chemicals involved this can make the boiling point of an azeotrope either higher *or* lower than either of the two components separately. In the case of water and ethanol the boiling point ends up at 172 degrees fahrenheit, which is lower than either of them on their own. This phenomenon happens with water and ethanol and occurs with ethanol and methanol too. The more methanol created in fermentation, the more it sticks to the ethanol and in this case its boilling point becomes higher. When fermenting with a lot of organic material—like, say, agave fibers—a lot of methanol is produced. Because of this, methanol is particularly pesky when distilling mezcal, and tends to exit the still later in distillation rather than sooner.

These chemical differences mean two things: first, mezcal has a bit more methanol in it than most other spirits. This additional methanol is no reason to be concerned because the amount that ends up in the bottle is very tightly regulated in certified mezcales. Secondly, this means the palenquero's decision on cutting the heads is more stylistic than pragmatic. It is based more on aromas and flavors than on a need to minimize methanol. There are a small handful of traditional producers that cut only tails, generally resulting in a more in-your-face and perfumey product.

The final step of making any spirit is a choice—to age or not to age? Tequila adopted its ideas on aging from the world-class luxury spirits it tried to emulate: Cognac and Scotch whiskey. Similarly tequila is often aged in small oak barrels or large wooden vats. In general, the length of time required to see an effect from aging depends on the climate where the aging is happening. Scotland is cold and clammy, and aging there takes a long time and progresses slowly. Kentucky is cold in the winter and hot in the summer, which speeds things up considerably. The tequila-producing regions are hot during the day and cold at night. This speeds up the process and results in the need for only very short periods of aging, from a few months to a few years.

The mezcal tradition never really included an oak aging component. Any barrel aging we see of mezcal is a parody of the practices seen in the tequila category. Some mezcal producers have hedged their bets and are operating under the assumption that international consumers will demand aged spirits. As a general rule oak-aged mezcal loses some of the pungent aroma and big personality that has made this spirit so uniquely attractive in the first place.

Distillation

Let's not mince words: fermentation and the agave itself receive top billing in the mezcal show. The only reason we aren't examining fermentation at greater length is that so much is simply unknown or unknowable about the process. Nature takes its course guided by the palenquero's hands, and we get to reap the benefits.

Distillation is essential to the creation of mezcal, though authorship is not counted among its powers. The still is an editing machine, allowing the palenquero to artfully pick and choose which flavors and aromas end up in the glass, and which get left behind. As we will see, there are also some extremely unique aspects to distilling in the mezcal world that are very much worthy of our attention. Compared to fermentation, it's a lot easier for us to know what's going on in the still, as distillation is the cornerstone of the contemporary pursuit of chemical engineering.

Fair warning: we're going to dive into some pretty heavy stuff. None of this is entirely crucial to our goal of getting our head around the subject of mezcal, but there are some juicy tidbits in here that help to bolster mezcal's reputation as the Qualitatively Best Spirit Category in the World. If you want to skip ahead to the next chapter, I promise I won't be mad.

We talked a bit last chapter about some of the main ideas behind distillation, and we did so from the perspective of an overview. Here we're diving deep into the how and why of distillation in general, before re-focusing our attention on what exactly this means for mezcal production.

Starting at the very beginning, things are heavy. Every molecule is made up of atoms, and each atom itself has a weight depending on how many protons and neutrons it has. That's basically what the periodic table is all about. Each molecule is made up of different types of atoms put in various configurations, and since they're all stuck together into one thing, they have the constituent weight of their atoms put together.

We said before that the still is an editing device, but editing is more the still's use than it is its function. The boiling point of a liquid is a complex thing, and is determined by not only the weight of the molecules that the liquid is made out of, but also how much those moecules like to chemically stick to one another. Fundamentally, think of a still as a separating-things-by-their-boiling-points device, and we use its separation abilities to edit what ends up in the bottle. This seems pretty straightforward, but there are few physical properties of liquids that throw this off a bit.

First off, let's look at evaporation. We all know that when we work out, our bodies sweat. That sweat evaporates, cooling us down. What's actually going on is a bit more complicated than that. All atoms are moving around all the time. Solids, liquids, and gases. Nobody knows what would happen if even one atom stopped moving entirely, and nature may be configured to prevent us from ever finding out. We think of this movement as temperature. The faster the atoms are moving, the hotter they are. As they knock around, they transfer heat to the other atoms near them, as your frying pan does to the bacon that's touching its surface.

When we sweat, our body covers itself with water. The molecules in the water are heated up by our perspiring bodies and knock into each other with the energy we radiate. When one molecule of water is near the surface and gets bumped into hard enough, it can convert from a liquid into a gas and break free of the water droplet. Doing this absorbs energy, which is what allows our bodies to use this as a way of cooling. The neat part is that water turned into a gas without reaching its boiling point. This is the same reason that if you leave a glass of water out for several days, it will continue to evaporate until it's empty. But wait, I thought that's what boiling was all about?

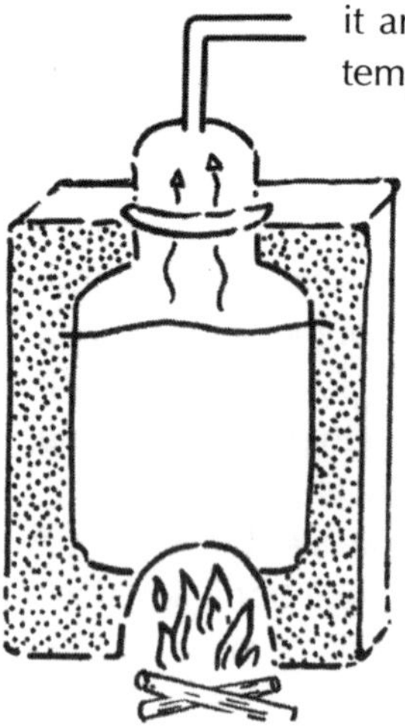

Boiling works in the same way, but the details surrounding it are just a tiny bit different. Boiling is the maximum temperature a liquid can be and still be a liquid, in relation to the atmospheric pressure surrounding it. It's like evaporation on steroids. The energy of the heated liquid knocks the molecules together very rapidly, turning the liquid into the gas as fast as possible. As we said before, the boiling point of water is higher than that of ethanol, making it way easier for us to use distillation to separate the two. If we heat the liquid up to above the boiling point of ethanol but below that of water, we're going to get a lot more ethanol vapor from boiling than water vapor from evaporation coming off the top. This is how we make spirits.

One final concept is essential for us, especially in the world of mezcal. Atomization is related to but very different than boiling or evaporation. Some liquids and most solids have very, very high boiling points. It's just simply not possible to get salt or sugar to boil without some extreme elemental stimulation. Also, a lot of times, solids like sugar will burn before they boil. Anybody out there ever screw up when making caramel? It tastes really, really nasty. Logic would seem to suggest to us that we're not going to see sugar or other heavy molecules evaporating in our still, no matter how high we turn up the heat.

Sometimes individual molecules of solids or liquids with very high boilling points can get knocked into the air and float around. Think like a snowflake. The process by which this happens is known as atomization, and it's the means by which sugars, lipids, waxes, and acids can end up in our mezcal. Another way to visualize it is fog. Fog is made up of liquid water particles suspended in the air. Steam is invisible, so if we can see it, we know the water in the air is still in liquid form.

Ok, so despite things being heavier and lighter, and those heavier and lighter things having different boiling points, pretty much anything can make it up and through our still. What does this leave us with? Chaos. Total chaos. Let's dive into an extended metaphor that will help us think about how a still is used by humans as a tool.

Let's imagine Powerball, America's favorite distributor of false hope. We have a container in which individually numbered balls are bouncing around. Each one is numbered one through fifty. If all the balls are the exact same, then there are equal odds that any one of them will be the first one to make its way to the top and be pulled by our lovely assistant. If our hypothetical lotto-still is filled only with water, any given water molecule could be the first to make it through.

Now, let's imagine that each ball increases in weight as its number increases. Ball three is heavier than ball two, which is heavier than ball one. This changes our odds quite a bit. We can't say for sure that ball number one is going to be the first one pulled, but we can say it's much more likely than ball number 50.

In our real world still, a very similar odds game is going on. By playing it smart and using the difference in boiling point between ethanol and water, we can drastically stack the odds in our favor, guaranteeing that we're going to receive more ethanol and lighter stuff through the still than we will H20. The odds are very unlikely in most applications that our lipids and sugars are going to break away and float through, relegating them to the tail end of distillation, if they break away at all.

This is an incredibly important point of distinction for mezcal among its spirit category contemporaries. With mezcal production, we have a ton of sugar and oil and acid in the mix, drastically more than is found when creating any other spirit. Because there's so damn much of the stuff, it increases the odds that some may come up through our still via atomization. This is why we get the body, sweetness, and acidity in the category of mezcal that we simply don't see anywhere else in the spirit world. Take that, bourbon.

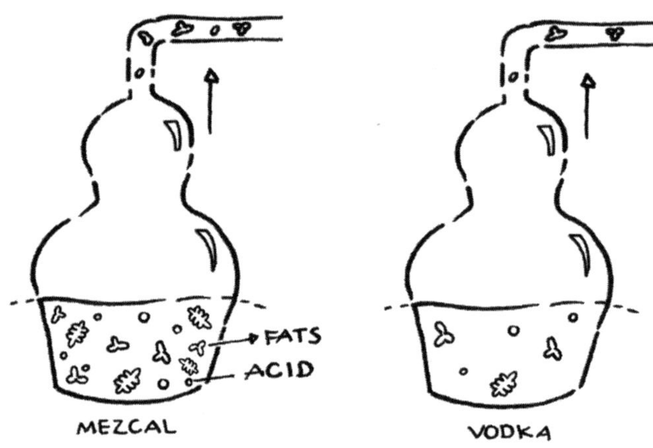

There's one other difficult-to-wrangle-with subject that needs some of our mental bandwidth. Some stills are more choosy than others. With distillation, we're playing an odds game, and depending on how the still is designed we can modify the odds overall.

Back to Powerball. Let's take our example from earlier but make one major change. The balls are still all increasing in weight from number one to number fifty, but this time we've changed the selection process just a bit. This time, instead of the first ball rising to the top being chosen, our lovely assistant drops the first three selected balls back in before finally taking the fourth one to rise to the top. For the next selection, our assistant will do the same, returning the first three and taking the fourth. While on the surface it may seem that we're facing the same odds situation as before, we've actually tweaked the statistics quite a bit. Remember, ball one is much more likely than ball 50 to rise to the top, so making the first selection after three rejections means that the odds that ball one will be the first selection and that ball fifty will be the last just got a whole lot better.

In distillation, we refer to this idea as efficiency, and it happens by rectification, a concept very similar to our Powerball metaphor. Through various means, the process of rectification is forcing some of the evaporated or atomized material in the still to condense and fall back down to the bottom of the still without making its way through and being collected with the finished product. This happens through a few different mechanisms.

Convection is one way. Convection is the process when a heated gas rises, cools, and then sinks back down. This creates currents inside the still that channel hot gas from the top down to the bottom where the still is filled with liquid. If water vapor, ethanol vapor, or atomized hitchhikers are trailing along for the ride, they'll find themselves back near the liquid-portion of the still and may end up turning back into or rejoining the liquid hanging out there.

Convection is a property of still design, as we'll soon investigate more closely. The other major way that stills vary in efficiency relates to condensation. If the vapor hits something cold and condenses, it will drip downwards in the still. If it lands on a collector or slides down the coil of the still, it ends up coming out where we collect the finished product. If not, it can drip back down in the still and rejoin the lotto to see what molecules make their way out the other side of the still.

OK, so we've got our heads around the forces at play and how they work, so let's dive into looking at the kit used to make mezcal and how it affects the final product. We'll start by looking at clay pot stills, and we'll look first at their major drawbacks. The first is an easy one to understand, clay is fragile and tends to break. We can only expect a clay pot still to have a certain duty cycle before it cracks and spills our precious liquid contents all over the place. This problem has a stop-gap solution, which is a problem in its own right. Palenqueros who use clay use multiple smaller stills instead of one large still. This means palenqueros lose less liquid in breakage, but it also means that distilling in clay is a bit more laborious than in copper.

Another significant drawback to clay is the design of the collector. In copper pot stills, vapors travel up and through the head, into the swan's neck, and down the lyne arm before condensing in a coil and being collected. In a clay pot still, this order is reversed. First, we condense with the pan of cool water on top of the still, and then we try to capture. The liquid drips down onto a collector in the middle of the still which is sometimes made from wood, sometimes made from a maguey leaf, sometimes made from whatever is available. From the collector, the liquid is channeled into a bamboo-like rod called a *carrizo,* which allows the liquid to drip out of the still. As we've heated up the liquid in the bottom of the still, this increases the pressure inside the still, causing some of the evaporated liquid to blow out of the carrizo in gas form. Because this tube is separate from the chiller, we lose these vapors as waste. To work properly, we have to throw away some of the alcohol we've made during fermentation.

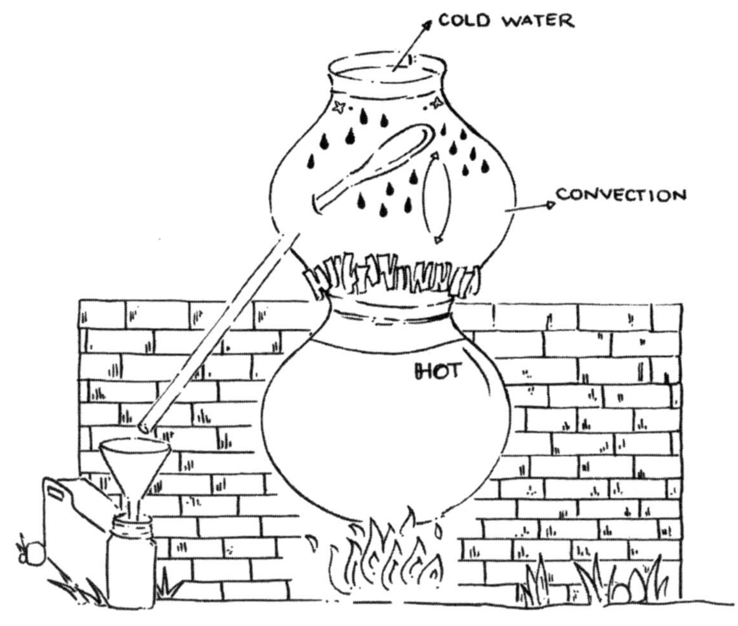

None of the drawbacks of using clay pot stills are desirable, but some pretty surprising advantages offset them. The rounded shape of the clay pot increases the amount of convection that happens inside the still, causing greater rectification and thus greater still efficiency. The pan of water used as the condenser also works in favor of greater rectification. The droplets of condensed liquid in the still often drop down onto the collector below, but many of them fall down the sides of the collector, allowing them to return to our distillation lotto. This makes for a surprising increase in rectifying efficiency, allowing clay pot stills to achieve a higher concentration of alcohol in the first distillation than their copper pot cousins.

Let's take a moment to bask in this. A still made out of earth and bamboo has a higher capacity for rectification than a standard copper pot still. A clay pot still was the most efficient means of distillation in terms of rectification until the invention of the continuous still in the early 20th century. Regardless of whether it emanated in the Americas or Asia, this is a testament to the inherent ingenuity of mezcal producers. The clay pot still may not look like much, but it is seriously advanced technologically.

The most obvious impact of a clay pot still is related to what it's made out of. Using earth to form a ceramic pot will allow our proto-mezcal to come in contact with any minerals present in the soil used. It's not always heavy-handed, but using a clay pot still can increase the minerality in a finished mezcal.

One last note on clay. The soil used to create the clay pots is chemically alkaline, which is to say the opposite of an acid. We've already mentioned several times that mezcal's fermented *tepache* is high in acidity. When heated at the bottom of the still and in contact with the basic clay, a catalytic reaction occurs, and as we know from high school chemistry class, an acid and a base react to form a chemical salt. This is not to say that this reaction creates a perceptible salinity in the finished product, but shows how the materials used to distill can create chemical differences during the distillation process.

As mentioned above, copper pot stills are generally better at capturing the alcohol vapors that they produce. They have the distinct advantage of condensing the vapors as the last step, with a great many opportunities for condensation given in the long serpentine condenser coil. When we distill with a copper pot still, we're simply throwing away less alcohol. All told though, a standard copper pot still is less efficient in rectification than our rustic clay pot.

In terms of material reactivity, copper is a strange beast. It does react with the liquid it contains during alcoholic spirits production, but only subtly. What little effect there is is increased if the heat to the still is applied by direct flame instead of steam. I've spoken to distillers and chemical engineers the world around, and I've yet to find anyone who can give me a concise explanation of what copper does during the creation of a distilled spirit. I've even encountered a rum producer who uses one single copper plate in a large stainless steel column still. Their explanation was murky, and revolved around the idea that "it just makes it better." Whatever the exact chemical relationship between distilled spirits and copper, it's out of the scope of our mission here.

There are a few very ingenuitive ways by which the efficiency of a copper pot still can be increased. Remember, the more likely rectification is to happen, the more efficient our still is going to get. With copper pot stills, the easiest way to do this is to chill the head of the still. This is done by running a large trough around the head and continually refilling it with cold water. The colder the water, the more vapor will come in contact with the head, spontaneously condense, and drip back down into the liquid below. This apparatus is known colloquially as a *resaque, refrescador, or refrescadera*. This type of tech finds a lot of use in the Oaxacan towns of Miahuatlán and Ejutla.

Additionally, the still's head can be modified to contain stripping plates. The idea of a plate in a still is akin to creating a second still within the still. Vapor must first make its way to the plate, where it re-condenses and must once again evaporate or atomize to proceed up higher. The plates are also designed so the condensed liquid has the chance to drip downward slowly. If a molecule is heavier, it is more likely that molecule will fall back down and start the process all over again. Mezcal producers who use plates in their stills tend to use two or three of them, though theoretically the head of the still can be made longer, more plates added, and the still made even more efficient.

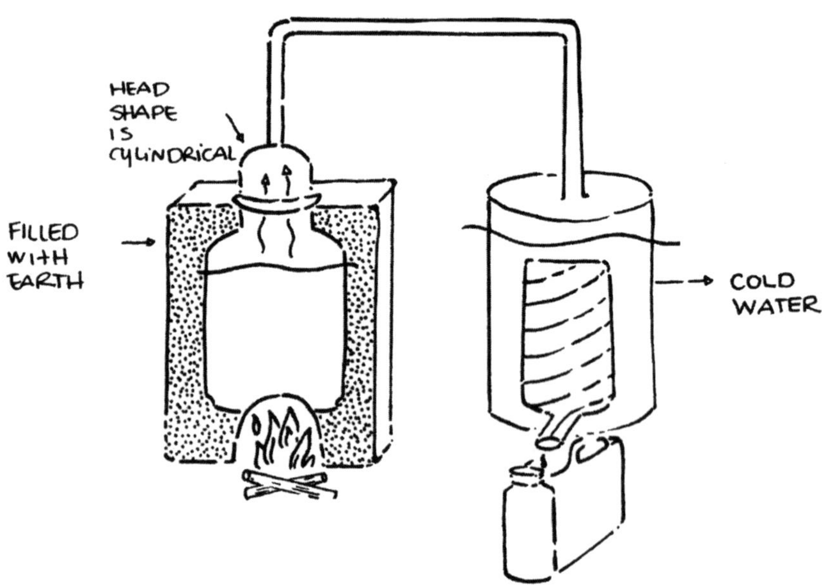

Palenqueros in the Oaxacan municipality of Ejutla most commonly use plates in combination with refrescadores, creating stills so efficient they can distill to the desired strength in just one pass. It's important to note that because of this extreme increase in efficiency, the mezcal production from Ejutla tends to be a bit lighter in body than other copper pot distillates. The odds just aren't in favor of heavier particles when a still is so extremely efficient.

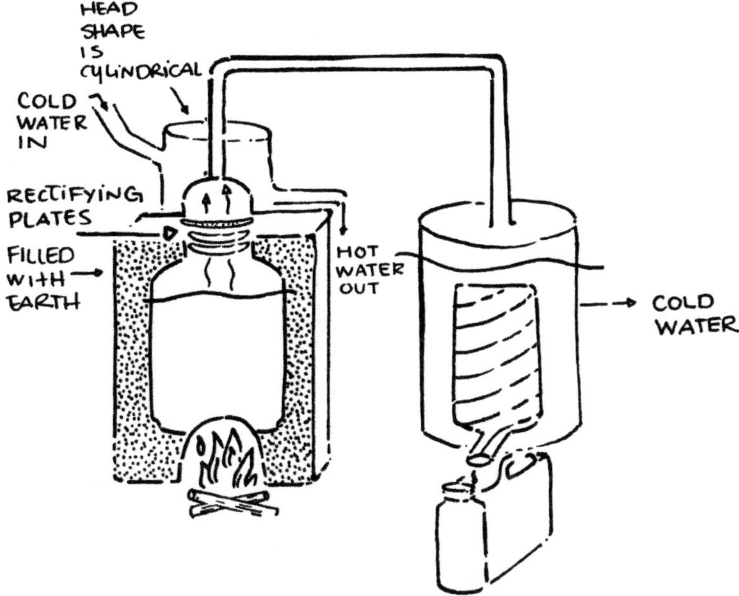

Ejutla Still Style

In Puebla, some producers have created what may be the most ingenuitive path towards a more efficient still that the world has ever seen.

On the back of every box of cake mix you'll find directions for preparing the cake normally and baking it at high altitude. There's nothing magic about being in the mountains. Being at a higher altitude means less atmospheric pressure, and lower atmospheric pressure causes liquids to boil at a lower temperature.

Remember sci-fi movies where people die when they get sucked out into space? It's not because they're bad at holding their breath. The total vacuum of space instantly takes all the air out of your lungs and causes the nitrogen in your blood to come out of solution almost immediately. The only reason your blood doesn't boil is that your skin is pretty good at keeping all your inner bits strapped together. Sounds... unpleasant. What's the point of all this? Differences in pressure have a huge impact on liquids and gasses.

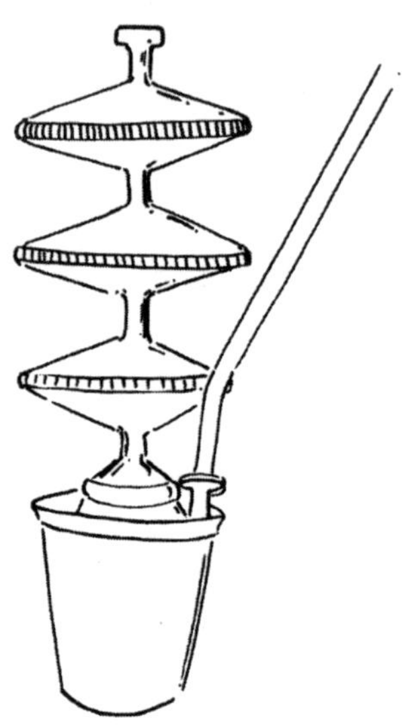

Puebla Still Style

The boiling point of a liquid lowers when there's less pressure. Producers in Puebla apparently understood this much better than anybody else. They produced a type of still, which they call a resaque, that made use of this pressure disparity to drastically increase still efficiency. This type of still has a series of expansion chambers in the head. The still bottlenecks down to a very small pipe, before quickly expanding out into a very wide bulb. This form repeats itself several times, creating areas of high pressure right before the bottlenecks and areas of low pressure where they expand out into bulbs. This device forces the gas passing through the still to compress, decompress, and then compress again multiple times. Each time this happens some of the gas condenses back into a liquid and falls back down to the bottom of the still. Just like in Ejutla, this reduces the odds that heavier elements will make their way to the condensing coil and ending up in the finished product.

Now we know the typical equipment that's used, but there are some crucial differences in still application that continue to differentiate mezcal in the world of spirits. Let's say we're making American whiskey using a copper pot still. The first distillation of our mash is mostly inconsequential. We can only raise the concentration of alcohol a certain amount in one distillation. Our first pass provides us the step up in the concentration of alcohol we need to make the leap to our final desired strength in our second distillation.

Once we start our second distillation, we need to pay considerable attention to making the cuts with whiskey and other spirits. What part of the distillate do we end up keeping and what do we discard? As the still heats up, the first liquid off for a whiskey contains a significant amount of methanol, and we don't want that to end up in the bottle. We let the still run until the majority of the nasties are gone, and then start capturing the spirit we intend to keep. We call that first portion the heads of the distillate. The product that continues running after the heads is referred to as the heart of the distillation, and it's the part we intend to keep. Eventually, the percentage of alcohol coming off the still will slowly drop, and with that drop also come heavier elements that we may not want in our finished product. This last portion of the distillation is known as the tails, and it gets left behind as well. For a whiskey, it's all about heart.

Mezcal is a contrarian spirit, and different technique is required to work with the fickle plant that is agave. As we said before, most of our methanol comes off at the very end of distillation, leaving us less to worry about in the heads department. As such, a different approach to cutting a distillation has evolved and requires an understanding of some different terminology.

The first liquid off the still often doesn't have a name, and there's not very much of it. Some palenqueros will pull off a small number of liters at the very beginning, and some won't even bother. This liquid can be discarded, used as a cleaning solvent, or consumed by the intrepid. Next, come the puntas, which can be loosely translated, confusingly, as heads. The puntas are the core of the distillation, and all told will end up being as high as 65% alcohol by volume. Puntas are aromatic and bright, with abundant flavor but little body or acid to write home about. To drink pure puntas is an intense but ethereal experience.

Once the ABV, or alcohol by volume, of the distillation begins to drop, the puntas are separated and set aside, and so start the *colas*, or tails. In whiskey parlance, this sounds a bit scary, but we're dealing with a very different plant as our starting point. The colas are run out of the still until the resultant liquid is about 20% to 30% alcohol, at which point we make another cut. What comes off after the colas is of little consequence and is mostly water, methanol, and undesirable flavors.

It's important to note that there are no hard and fast definitions of any parts of the distillation. While one producer divides from the first drop of distillation into puntas and colas, another producer may divvy their distillate up into the unnamed first cut of a few liters, then puntas, then the heart or *corazón*, the subsequent colas, and then lastly the unnamed feints at the tail end. Two parts, three parts, or five parts, it all depends who's at the helm of the still and whose hand guides the distillation process. For simplification, we'll be looking at a hypothetical distillation in which no cut is made in between puntas and colas.

Next up comes a part in the process that's a bit different than other spirits, the *ajuste*, or adjustment. For the ajuste, there are options. The palenquero can take the puntas and cut them with pure water to bring the mezcal down to the desired proof. They can also choose to use the colas to do so instead, or do a combination of both. The colas do contain quite a bit of alcohol, which is why we're making mezcal in the first place. It may sound like a purely economic move to use colas to adjust, but remember what we said before. Flavor, aroma, body, acidity, and sweetness are abundant in the colas, and they're collectively the real prize here, not just booze.

Using the right amount of colas to adjust a mezcal is an artful process by which palenqueros can maximize the flavor of the spirit. The use of colas also helps to explain the funky proof-points at which mezcal is often bottled. 405 liters of 62% puntas plus 201 liters of 21% colas gets us a respectable 48.4% alcohol for our finished product. This is by no means to say that adjusting a mezcal with colas is the only proper way to go. The distillation style in Ejutla doesn't produce a colas cut, meaning that adjusting with water is the only option.

The use of colas can be an economic consideration as well. If bottling a cocktail mezcal at 40% alcohol is in the goal, the more colas that can be used the less money is left on the table. Ideally, the palenquero is in control of the adjustment process and is proceeding with quality in mind. Regardless, this crucial step is the final element of authorship, and once again differentiates mezcal as the most unique spirits category in existence.

Agave Types

Wine is the shining star of the comparative tasting world. People have been analyzing Bordeauxs and talking about the vintages of German riesling for well over a hundred years. The center of the discussion, or the end goal of the blind tasting, always circles around varietal. Grapes have a rich diversity of expressions, and the triumvirate of soil, climate type, and cultivar make the wine world so diverse.

From a distance, it seems that mezcal is cut from this very same cloth. Different varieties of plants and variation in the process result in differences from one production to the next. As a metaphorical comparison, this works well. There are, though, some substantial differences that set agaves apart as a starting point for spirits.

Vitis vinifera is the species of grape most frequently used to make wine, and under its umbrella lie all the greatest hits of the wine world: cabernet sauvignon, pinot noir, chardonnay, nebbiolo, gewürztraminer, and just about any other varietal that comes to mind. All of them are the same species, much as all dogs are the same species as one another. At a base level, many of the agave varietals that we encounter in the mezcal world are different species, though they all share the same genus of *Agave*.

Dr. Ivan Saldaña Oyarzábal is a world renowned expert on agaves and agave spirits. He has a Ph.D. in Plant Biology/Biochemistry from the University of Sussex, is the co-founder of his own mezcal brand, and put out one of the most succinct books on mezcal to date, *The Anatomy of Mezcal*. Much of his research surrounds the biological functions of agaves, and he's given various talks and seminars outlining some of the factors that make agaves special for making booze. According to Ivan, agaves produce a wealth of chemicals which have flavor and aroma. Important among these are terpenes, saponins, esters, and essential oils. Many of these chemicals have evolved as defensive mechanisms to prevent predators big, small, and microscopic, from taking advantage of the agave's convenient energy stores. Terpenes are chemicals that tend to have strong, herbacious aromas, and some species of agaves contain around 30 different terpenes that can survive the roasting and distillation process. One important terpene found in agave is vanilin, the chemical responsible for vanilla's distinctive aroma.

Agave spirits are a daunting category in general. Different options in production technique, especially when combined with the unfathomable complexity of wild fermentation, create a mathematically overwhelming number of potential outcomes. Factoring in the wealth of species and variants of agave plants only makes this landscape more complex. As a mezcal consumer, it's easy to understand how the overwhelming number of agave names and types tends to be among the hardest aspects to understand and keep straight.

In a bar setting, this often results in guests resorting to the tactic of "pour me what you like" or "pour me a good one." It's always worthy of re-stating that there is no wrong way to approach this subject matter. Enthusiasm and good intention are the greatest potential assets that any consumer of mezcal can possess. That being said, the first thing to embrace is the idea that different mezcales offer different flavor profiles and appeal to people for various reasons.

The more information you can give to your bartender about the types of flavors you like in general, the better results you'll get when it comes time for them to help you find something to sip on. After a while, you'll begin to understand the personalities of different agave types and which ones may speak well to you personally. What we'll set out to do here is to give you a bit of a cheat-sheet for trying to understand the different flavors and characteristics that tend to come from each agave type.

But first, some housekeeping. Instead of getting deeply bogged down with the hundreds of various names used to describe these majestic plants, we will instead treat only the most commonly used, and will do so broadly. Understand that in the world of mezcal there is an exception to almost every rule. You'll find some degree of crossover in nomenclature, which far from being a typo is reflective of regional, local, or sometimes familial traditions.

Herein we attempt to tether our grasp of agave types to scientific names, even though the field of taxonomy is far from conclusive or complete. You'll note that some agave types share common names with other not-so-biologically-similar agave types. It is relatively commonplace for an agave to be locally called by a name which describes how it looks or how it grows. If it's somewhat gray in color, it'll likely be called *'cenizo,'* or ashen. If it's green or yellow compared to other local varieties, it may pick up the names *'verde'* or *'amarillo'* respectively. Knowing where we are geographically will help us understand which name refers to which scientific species. A cenizo in Michoacán is likely to be an *Agave americana,* while one in Durango it's likely a reference to a *durangensis.*

Nature knows no artificial bounds. Just because it says below that a given type of agave lives in one specific spot, that is in no way exhaustive. We're speaking in generalities here to make as much sense of the situation as we can. We're also talking about flavor generalities, a foolhardy pursuit. If I say tobalá tends to produce flavors like candy corn and Robitussin, we're most definitely over-generalizing.

Also, we'll be talking a bit about genetics vs. morphology. We're broadly defining genetics as the biological disposition of the plant. When we use the term morphology, we're looking at the form into which the mature plants grow. If the plant almost always grows in the same way, we'll talk about it being morphologically consistent. If it grows into various forms in different places, we'll be talking about morphological variation. Note that it's impossible for us to tell the exact reasons for variation in plants, but it's safe to assume that when we talk about morphology, we're not excluding the influence of genetics in any way. Likely the culprit is a bit of column A and a bit of column B.

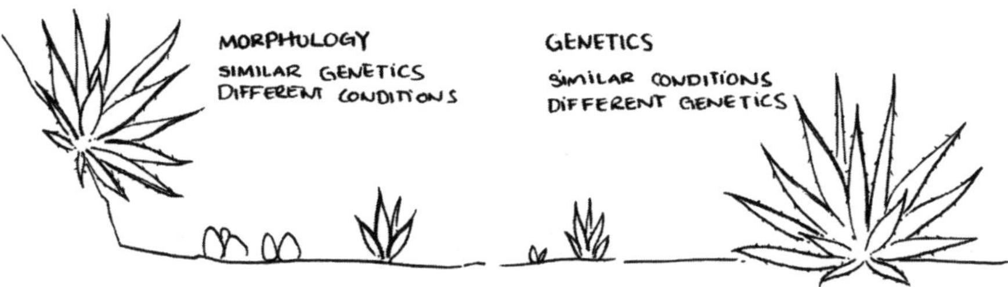

Within certain species, looking at morphology will tell us how much flavor variation we should expect from mezcales made from a given species. Genetics help us to know more about the cross-compatibility of different species, and how likely we are to see the line between the two species become a bit blurry.

Lastly, thoughts on age. As every Red Blooded American knows, more is better. The fastest car, the most expensive watch, the oldest cognac. Superlative is directly equal to quality. Many educators fixate on the age range in which an agave species comes into maturity as though this is a vital statistic. Understanding the general age range of agave species at best can inform us of how the specific varieties of plants grow, and at worst can be used as a comparative factor to indicate which species are "better."

It's also worthy of note that palenqueros don't individually track these plants for age and maturity in sprawling spreadsheets. Most often the age of the plant at harvest is estimated. I spoke to one palenquero who was unloading *Agave karwinskii*s from his truck to transplant them in his fields at a later time. The plants were roughly a foot and a half long, with the leaves trimmed down to remove their spines and make them easier to handle. When I asked how old the plants were, the response I received was "these are three years, but if I were selling them to you they'd be five." Equal parts light-hearted nod and cautionary message to the nature of relying on the numbers as a sign of quality.

Regardless of age or reputation, the absolute best agave type to enjoy in mezcal form is simply the one which speaks to you. Some people prefer the piney green notes of *agave marmorata*, while others dig the soft sweetness and spice of an *angustifolia*. I think you'll be served best in general by drinking what you like, not what you're told is the best.

Agave angustifolia

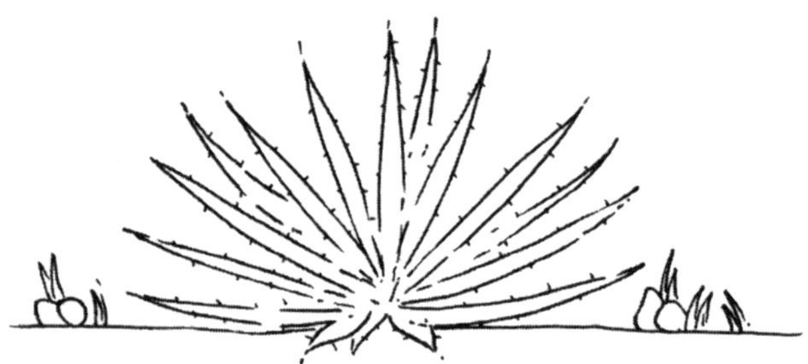

Names:
Espadín, espadílla, Weber blue agave, bacanora, castilla, pacifica.

Distribution:
From Sonora across to Tamaulipas, all the way down to Costa Rica.

Size and Physical Description:
While ornamental variants of *Agave angustifolia* can often be quite small, cultivated angustifolia is usually on the larger side. The plants are often 5 to 7 feet in height and feature a sizeable, sugar-rich piña at the center. Their coloration varies from the eponymous blue tones of Weber blue agave to the more subdued greenish-blue seen in fields and on hillsides all over Oaxaca.

If we ever hope to understand mezcal, we best familiarize ourselves with *A. angustifolia* first and foremost. This trusty plant is the most commonly employed for making spirits for good reason. *A. angustifolia* takes well to agriculture, grows relatively quickly, produces a high sugar yield, and provides numerous offsets. It's adaptable to various soil types and growing conditions, making for a utility player of the highest order. At the moment, distillates made from agave espadín represent the vast majority of mezcal available today.

Due to its abundant sugar yield, less agave can be used to create more spirit, and as such its flavor palate is more general than specific. The roasted piñas of *A. angustifolia* are rich in flavors reminiscent of baking spices and squash. Think of this as the baseline flavor set for roast agave in general, with different species molding this form by bringing more flavors and aromas to the table.

Agave angustifolia is unique in its current position as one of the very few agave species that are primarily cultivated for spirits production. That being said, wild espadín is occasionally used to make mezcal or other agave spirits. The frequent use of offsets to grow Agave *angustifolia* for agriculture has resulted in a monoculture taken to the extreme. Not only are plants very genetically similar and thus susceptible to the same sorts of pests and blights, but often the plants are genetically identical.

Nowhere is this easier to see than in the blue agave fields of Jalisco. The tequileros have for a long time preferred growing their *angustifolia* the fast way, and as such genetic variation is at an all-time minimum. These practices are not uncommon anywhere *angustifolia* is cultivated, but the scale of growth efforts for tequila has resulted in an unprecedentedly risky monocultural crop.

This fully illustrates both the potential benefit and the risks of agave agriculture. Regardless of what product it's being grown to produce, genetic variation must be reintroduced to Agave *angustifolia*. Failure to do so will put at risk entire crops as well as the livelihood of many who depend on these rugged plants.

Agave potatorum

Names:
Tobalá, papalometl, papalome.

Distribution:
Oaxaca and Puebla.

Size and Physical Description:
Agave potatorum tends to be around 1.5 to 2.5 feet in diameter. There are larger variants in Puebla, but the genetic lines between *potatorum* and *cupreata* get a bit blurry there as there is some genetic cross-compatibility. *Potatorum's* coloration is bluish gray to grayish green, and the plant often has a fat, conical terminal spine and pronounced marginal spines on the leaves.

Age range: 8-15

Often mythologized, *Agave potatorum* is highly sought-after for making mezcal. It is a smaller agave that grows a bit more slowly than some other species. *Agave potatorum* is found throughout Oaxaca and into Puebla but grows extensively in the foothills of the Sierra Norte and la Mixteca Alta. It tends to produce sweeter, nutty and buttery flavors, and generally offers a bit more complexity than agave espadín. Some have said that *Agave potatorum* can only be found in the shade of oak trees, claiming the plants have a mythical and mysterious connection to where they choose to grow. In reality, biology has a lot to do with where *potatorum* ends up. Far from being controlled by a supernatural force, the physical distribution of *Agave potatorum* is a cunning evolutionary response to a unique quandary.

As mentioned before, *A. potatorum* grows very slowly. As a mature plant it also rarely creates offsets. As such, the plant relies almost entirely on growing to maturity and cross-pollinating. Once pollinated, the wind disperses its seeds and so begins an odds game; which seeds will grow to maturity and which will succumb to competition.

Much of Oaxaca experiences a distinct rainy season and a prolonged dry season. Rainy season happens during summer, with under half the year seeing consistent rainfall. The remainder of the year is extremely dry, posing two sets of disparate challenges for plants. The first challenge is to germinate and grow as soon as water is available. The second challenge is to grow enough during the rainy season and save enough resource to make it through the heat and drought of the rest of the year until rain once again begins to fall.

Various types of plants have varying strategies to cope with these challenges. *Agave potatorum* takes the slow and steady route. Once their seeds germinate, they grow much more slowly than surrounding plants. As such, any seeds that fall in rich soil tend to be choked out by other types of plants that grow much more quickly. While at first this seems like an extreme disadvantage, it's all part of the *A. potatorum* plan. *A. potatorum* is a bit of a specialist, and its sights are not set on rich soil or such areas of extreme competition.

When the wind disperses its seeds, they will sometimes encounter areas that other plants find to be uninhabitable. Dry, dusty crags on the side of sheer cliff faces are where one often sees *Agave potatorum* in the wild. Their seeds finding their way into such forlorn spaces is what they've evolved specifically to do. Given the relative absence of surrounding soil, the *potatorum* seed will face little to no competition once it germinates. The crags on cliff faces are also relatively good at holding water during rainy season. Like most agave types, the seeds of *Agave potatorum* need to be thoroughly soaked in water to start the germination process. The small crevices on cliff faces catch and hold water during rain, making them an ideal place for *potatorum* to sprout and grow.

The more out-of-the-way or unlikely the spot, the greater the chance is that a tobalá seed may find its way there and set up shop. This has helped to stoke the mythological status of these plants and further enshrine their reverence among both palenqueros and consumers. Their slow growth, fickle nature, and sought-after status have conspired to make *Agave potatorum* particularly worrisome when it comes to their natural ecosystem and the conservation thereof.

All around Oaxaca I've encountered efforts to tame and domesticate *Agave potatorum,* and I'm optimistic about the future of agave agriculture in general. By allowing the seeds to grow in a controlled environment with no competition, they can grow in size and be transplanted to hillsides and fields alike. I've even seen successful growth efforts in the lush Sierra Norte, where competition from other plants is extreme. Whether this difference in the environment will affect the flavor of the resultant mezcal, only time will tell.

Agave karwinskii

Names:
Madrecuixe, Cuixe, Bicuixe, Largo, Barril, tobasiche.

Distribution:
Southern Mexico, specifically Oaxaca.

Size and Physical Description:
A. Karwinskiis grow up more than they grow out and as such reach heights of 8-15 ft. tall. *Agave karwinskii's* leaves have a warm green cast, making them stand out when cultivated alongside the slightly bluish hues of *A. angustifolia* and *A. americana*.

Age range: 7-20

Botany is one of the few pursuits in life where one can take personal credit for hundreds of thousands of years of evolutionary forces. Named after his contemporary Wilhelm Friedrich Karwinski, *Agave karwinskii* was first scientifically described by botanist Joseph Gerhard Zuccarini in 1833.

Agave karwinskii has a striking feature that allows us to identify it with relative ease when compared to other agave types: it grows tall, like a very short tree. Most agave types grow in size radially, with each leaf pushing out and downward as the other, larger leaves underneath it continue growing. This results in the heart of the agave being relatively round in shape. Agave *karwinskii* grows upwards in layers, producing a piña that is oblong and skinny.

Agave karwinskii has a broad spectrum to its morphological variation. On one end of the spectrum are *Agave karwinskiis* that tend to grow more quickly and produce fewer sugars. These types of expressions are often referred to by the local names agave cuixe, largo, and tobasiche. The leaves of these variants tend to die out towards the bottom of the plant, leaving behind their dried stumps as the piña. The piña at the base of the plant is often so dry that it could easily be mistaken for the trunk of a tree.

The leaves above this bottom section terminate in the upper part of the piña, which tends to be small and skinny. Once cut down and trimmed, the true shape of the piña is fully revealed: its form looks not unlike a wiffle ball bat. The thicker part of the piña has very little sugar, and the stumpy bit below it even less. The roasted piña has a high acidity and a bitter, coffee-like bass note. The palenquero can either use the entire piña together or remove the stumpy bit, as it contains more of these bitter flavors.

Because of its low sugar content, the cuixe, largo, or tobasiche-variant karwinskiis require a lot of plant matter to make the same amount of mezcal. This means that tart, bitter, and earthy flavors found in these agave types are more likely to make it through distillation and end up in the finished product. It's not uncommon for these less-ripe karwinskiis to produce dark and earthy flavors.

The other end of the morphological karwinskii spectrum is often referred to as madrecuixe, bicuixe, or barril depending on the producer and the location. These karwinskiis develop more slowly and amass more sugars during their growth. Their leaves stay lush, growing all the way from the top of the plant to the ground. Their piñas grow larger in diameter and contain more sugar than compared to their less-ripe siblings. This results in greater yield than the underripe *karwinskii* variants and far less bitter and earthy flavors. It is also more common that the entire agave piña will be used to produce mezcal.

Mezcales made from the more-ripe *karwinskii* variants trend towards brighter, fruitier, and sometimes nutty flavors. The variants referred to as madrecuixe often produce flavors of peanuts and milk chocolate. Regardless of the characteristics of the specific products, the more ripe *karwinskiis* taste substantially different than their less-ripe siblings.

While we're not able to separate out genetic factors from environmental ones, we can try to understand a bit about why there's such variation among *karwinskiis.* Let's say I told you you had won the lottery, and you'd get a check every Friday for the rest of your life. In scenario one, you will receive $200 every week. While not a life-changing amount of money, it's certainly a benefit. One might decide to save that money, little by little contributing to their overall financial plan. One would hardly use this as an excuse to throw fiscal caution to the wind.

In scenario two, you get a check every week for ten grand till the end of your days. As you now know your financial future is eternally optimistic, you may choose to indulge yourself and go on a non-stop spending spree. Your concern over how much is in your bank account at any given point in time is diminished by your knowledge that the future is going to be bright no matter what.

While not the only factor contributing to their growth patterns, this chain of logic plays a factor with *Agave karwinskii.* Agaves as plants can sometimes have counterintuitive responses to their environmental conditions. If the plants have worse access to water and soil resources, they may be more likely to save their energy for the future. If they have greater access to resources, they may squander what they have, knowing they do not fear for their security.

Just like human economics, too much stress can cause the exact opposite result. If a person makes too little money, they won't be able to save at all. Stress and the role it plays in agave development has a tipping point. If the plant has too little resource, it may grow underdeveloped or die.

Given constant growing conditions, an individual *karwinskii* will save more or less sugar based on the plant's energy storage strategy and its genetic predisposition. Using the word ripeness to describe this phenomenon is only for lack of a better term, as an agave cuixe will come to sexual maturity without ever producing as much sugar as an as-of-yet immature madrecuixe.

Agave marmorata

Names:
Tepextate, Tepestate, Pichometl, Pichomel.

Distribution:
From central Oaxaca, stretching widely towards Jalisco along the Pacific coast, and up into Puebla.

Size and Physical Description:
Often slightly wider than it is tall, *Agave marmorata* reaches upwards of 5 feet in height and 6.5 feet in diameter. It is usually yellowish green and can be easily identified by its gnarly, thick leaves bearing the imprints of its large marginal spines. The spines are typically dark brown or red and stand out in stark contrast to the leaves.

Age range: 15-35

Agave marmorata is a species famed and mythologized for its long life and slow growth. Many age estimates range upwards of 35 years, though the plant can reach maturity in under 20 years depending on conditions and genetics. *Agave marmorata* has pencas with thicker-than-average cuticles. This thick, waxy cuticle presents a problem to mezcal production. As such it's common to shave the piña of *marmorata* all the way down to its base to prevent this surplus of fats and waxes from having a negative impact on the resultant mezcal. Regardless, the construction of the plant imparts an unmistakable green flavor element on its mezcales. Depending on region and genetic variation, *marmorata* prefers to reproduce by seed or bulbil offset, giving off only a handful of regular offsets over its long life. *Agave marmorata* exhibits a low amount of morphological variation, resulting in relatively consistent nomenclature regionally and a relatively consistent starting point for the creation of mezcal.

Agave americana

Names:
Arroqueño, Coyote, Blanco, Sierra Negra.

Distribution:
Ranges widely in Mexico, with concentrations along the South Pacific coast.

Size and Physical Description:
Agave americana generally ranges from 5 to 10 feet tall. It's been bred into various ornamental forms which are seen all around the world, thought the varieties employed to make mezcal share a similar color to agave angustifolia, a bluish-green.

Age range: 5-30

Agave americana is the archetypal image of the agave genus for much of the world. It's classic form succinctly demonstrates the key features which define agave as a genus. This was not lost on botanists. The species was first described by Carl Linnaeus, the guy who created the Linnaean system which we use to this day.

Agave americana has a host of morphological variation which results in creating mezcales with drastically different flavor profiles. Mezcales made from the diminutive agave coyote often are deep and dark, while those produced from agave arroqueño, the largest and slowest growing of the bunch, trend towards piquant and green. Agave coyote matures among the quickest, coming of age in as few as five years, while arroqueño can take upwards of 20 to 25 years to reach sexual maturity.

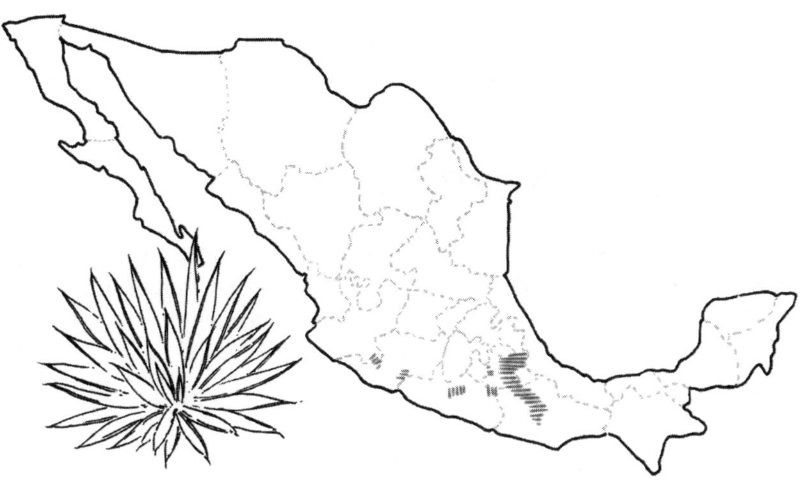

Agave rhodacantha

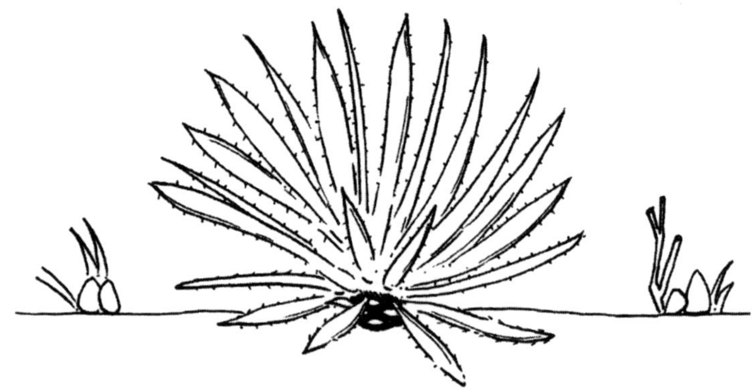

Names:
Mexicano, Cuixe (in Santa Catarina Minas), Ixtero Amarillo.

Distribution:
Agave rhodacantha ranges widely along the south Pacific coast of Mexico.

Size and Physical Description:
Rhodacantha grows to generally 4 to 7 feet in height, often being just smaller than agave espadín. It's coloration and leaf construction are similar too, with its numerous leaves baring hues slightly more yellow-tinged in comparison.

Age range: 8-15

One could be forgiven for mistaking a cut *rhodacantha* piña for that of a strange *karwinskii. Rhodacantha* is one of few species which grows up in addition to out, though this is not nearly as ostensible when looking at the plant as it grows. Once cut and trimmed, the piña often has a short, stalky trunk which flares out into a bulbous round shape piña. *Agave rhodacantha* generally results in mezcales with distinct, fiery spice. This piquancy is a love-it-or-hate-it type characteristic.

Agave cupreata

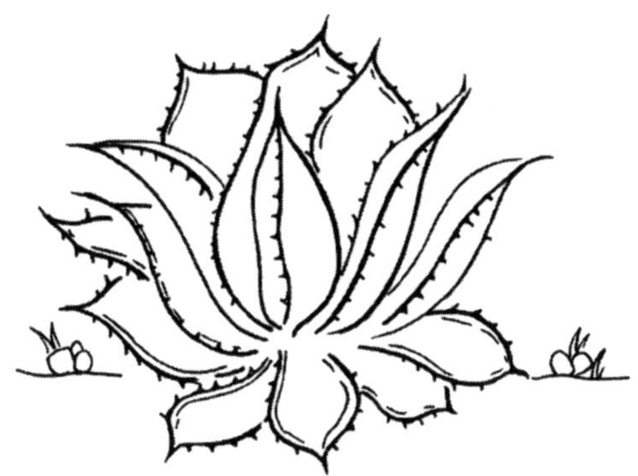

Names:
Papalote, Papalometl.

Distribution:
Mexico's south Pacific coast.

Size and Physical Description:
Though typically they tend to be small, around 3-4 feet tall, variants of *Agave cupreata* can grow rather large. With numerous thin, wide pencas one would be forgiven for mistaking cupreata for a slightly larger *Agave potatorum*. Generally, *cupreata* has a less conical terminal spine in comparison.

Age range: 8-15

Agave cupreata grows wild throughout central and southern Mexico. It is frequently harvested and made into mezcal in Michoacán, Guerrero, and Oaxaca's western Mixteca Alta region. *Agave cupreata* often shares earthy, gritty, mineral-driven characteristics with other varietal mezcales produced in these regions. A significant degree of genetic compatibility between *cupreata* and *potatorum* has led to cross-pollination and hybridization, especially in the mountains of Puebla.

Agave durangensis

Names:
Cenizo, Verde, Blanco.

Distribution:
Northern and Central Mexico, specifically the states of Durango and Zacatecas.

Size and Physical Description:
Hearty and spry, *Agave durangensis* bears some physical similarity to *Agave cupreata*, though with far fewer leaves emanating from its piña. Its leaves often bear the imprints of the plant's spines, and they grow from 4 to 6 feet in height and diameter.

Age range: 8-15

Mezcal has been made in Northern Mexico for generations, though only recently has it become available outside of the region. It's no surprise that *Agave durangensis* is found mostly in the Northern state of Durango, and mezcales created from this varietal tend to produce earthy and mineral flavors indicative of the region's arid terroir.

Agave salmiana

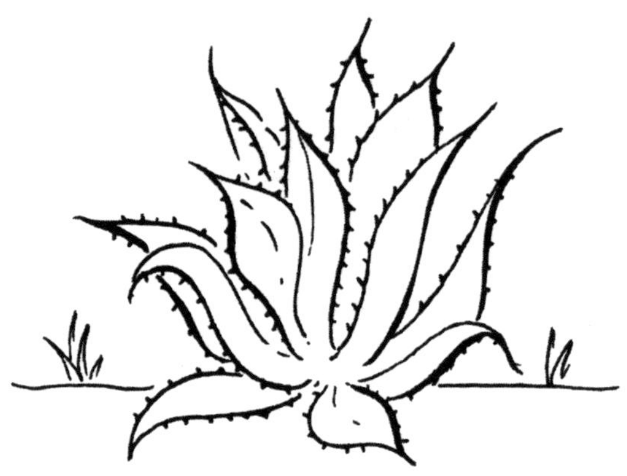

Names:
Cenizo, Verde, Amarillo, Pulquero.

Distribution:
Central and Southern Mexico, with large wild populations in San Luis Potosí.

Size and Physical Description:
Agave salmiana can look a bit like *agave marmorata*. It too has big thick leaves but can be identified by a few distinct details. The leaves of *agave salmiana* tend to be a bit more numerous, and its marginal spines tend to blend in just a bit more against the greenish hues of its leaves.

Age range: 10-20

Agave salmiana has an important role in the history of making booze from agave. *Salmiana* the most frequently employed of several types of larger agaves commonly used by humans to produce pulque. It grows wild in large numbers in San Luis Potosí and has a notable amount of morphological variation. This has resulted in it being regionally called by various descriptive names, though in Oaxaca it's most commonly referred to as agave pulquero.

Most mezcales being produced today tend to be made from a single agave varietal. Espadín comprises most mezcal made for cocktails, as well as many excellent expressions for sipping. Single-varietal mezcales made from more rarified agave types command hefty price tags and are often saved for special occasions or moments of indulgence. Some may be surprised to learn that this wasn't always the case.

Several hundred years ago mezcal was more about necessity than dégustation. It was made to be consumed and traded, and getting around wasn't terribly easy back then. Agave agriculture was in its infancy, and there were more than enough plants growing wild to satisfy the needs of palenqueros. The agave that was nearby and ripe was harvested and produced together into a batch of mezcal, with often the composition of varietals used changing from batch to batch. This style of mezcal is still produced by some today. It's known by the name *mezcal del campo,* or in English, a field blend. These are often labeled by brands as *ensembles,* but this term finds its origins in French, not Spanish.

These types of mezcal offer a window into the spirits consumed hundreds of years ago, and perhaps, more importantly, they're very hard to pin down. The very Western desire to analyze things, to organize them into neat buckets governed by strict rules, breaks down when we venture into the realm of mezcales del campo. While we strive to memorize the characteristics that typify a tobalá or arroqueño, we're often missing the point. Palenqueros create mezcal to be enjoyed, to be shared, and to be experienced. Drinking a mezcal del campo adds so many pieces to the puzzle that it's incredibly hard to track down the exact provenance of flavor and aroma in the glass. Being too systematic and methodical poses the very real risk of screwing up what could otherwise be a very good time.

Economic Realities

We've now taken a pretty thorough look under the hood of the process of making mezcal. It's a different beast than most other spirits on the planet, and more often than not this incredible liquid is made in pretty rustic circumstances and incredibly intuitive ways. Without the insane surplus of ingenuity demonstrated by the average palenquero, making a spirit in this way would be foolhardy at best and disastrous at worst.

The roots of the international mezcal explosion are firmly planted in an informal economy of generations-deep spirits producers and intra-community transactions. For hundreds of years, people in rural Mexico have shod horses, built home-spun irrigation systems, raised livestock, and made spirits. The needs of the community were primarily served by its members, and barter, exchange, and monetary transactions made this happen.

At its very best, mezcal is a window into a life ruled by tradition. A father teaches his son to make mezcal exactly how he learned from his father before him. The mezcal that they make is revered and enjoyed by their community and allows the family to make ends meet. Through intuition and trial and error the family has taken a raw material that's hard to work with and crafted it into something beautiful. The importance of the mezcalero in rural Mexico is not to be underestimated. More than just a commodity, mezcal is the fuel for all of life's biggest events.

Outsiders who have taken a shine to mezcal often try to position themselves as a fly on the wall. We crave the ability to share in these traditions at a distance and enjoy a consumable window into another world. All folks who sell liquor try to tout their wares as something special, but the importance of mezcal to these communities trumps any limited release or gimmicky promo that international spirits companies can conjure up. This is the big picture promise of mezcal as a category. As a consumer, you get a seat at the table of tradition while your money goes to fund the future of those who make mezcal and by proxy their communities.

This is the true promise of mezcal. Families reunited as sons and daughters return from sojourns in the US to help their families run their burgeoning businesses. The money from the sale of mezcal trickling into Mexico from the ground up, helping first those who need it the most. It's a tale of capitalism that Horatio Alger would be proud of.

It's unfortunate, but the reality is quite a bit more complicated than that. There have been a few major paradigm shifts that have altered the course of the history of mezcal and molded the economics surrounding its sale. We'll get to those in the next chapter, but first we have to look at some fundamental sociological realities that impact where the profits of internationally-sold mezcal end up.

Economics might not seem like the most enthralling subject, but understanding a few things about cultural economic perspective is crucial to understanding the state of mezcal. It's easy to assume one's economic perspective is the same as everyone else's. What do I mean when I say economic perspective? Broadly, this concerns matters of monetary fairness. How much of a company's profit should go to the CEO, and how much to the factory worker? While these things get highly contentious in specific, defining one's perspective is a lot easier in broader strokes.

As not to make assumptions about you, dear reader, I'll be walking through this from my personal perspective. I was born in the United States, and I was raised to believe certain things about the nature of money and work. The ideology in which I was raised could broadly be called western capitalism. The capitalistic perspective is that innovation and hard work beget individual profit and success. Let's say my neighbor and I both start lawn care businesses. If I go out every day and knock on doors, hustle, and spend long hours operating a weed whacker (always with eye protection), then capitalism dictates that I deserve to make a profit for doing so. If my neighbor spends her days slacking off instead of doing work, a capitalist would suggest that maybe she doesn't deserve the profit that I make.

There's another concept closely tied to capitalism - the idea of voting with one's dollars. In the scenario above, the others in my neighborhood might have several reasons to solicit my services over those of my competition. One reason is that it is more likely that I will perform the services they've paid for—I'm probably going to show up—whereas my competitor may decide she should take the day off instead. There's also an implication that my motivation will lead to me doing a better job. I'm motivated by the profit that I stand to make, while my neighbor seems indifferent to it. My customers assume that I will try not only to earn their payment once, but that my motivation for profit will cause me to do a good job so as to convince them to hire me again. Lastly, if my customers share my capitalistic mindset, they too believe that my motivation makes me deserving of profit. Oddly, they feel *good* about giving their money to me, even though they know that not all of it goes to cover my costs. By allowing me to make a profit, they feel like they're supporting me in my quest to make a better life for my family and me. They've chosen to place their funds in my ballot box versus that of my competitor, and simultaneously feel like they're rewarding me and punishing her.

Chances are a lot of you reading this will find this to be a very familiar notion. The core tenants of western capitalism have spread all over the world. Even in nominally communist countries, free markets are alive and well. It may come as some small shock to most that there exist societies that do not subscribe to these tenants as firmly as we do, if at all.

Mexico is a nation formed out of a great coming together, *un mestizaje*. One of the things that makes Mexico so unique is the vast gradient of cultures, starting at the great many pre-hispanic societies on one end, and arriving at the Spaniards on the other. This cultural gradient is alive and well and means that different influences are stronger or weaker based on ethnic background and geography.

In rural Oaxaca these indigenous roots are strong. Many villages in the Valle Central are Spanish speaking, but venturing off into the mountains there are many villages where Zapotec, Mixtec, or Mixe might be the primary language. With language comes custom and cultural ideal. In rural Oaxaca ideas about how society should work stem significantly from their Mesoamerican forebearers.

Phil Dahl-Bredine and Stephen Hicken did a wonderful job treating the specifics of non-western cultural influence in Oaxaca in their book *The Other Game - Lessons from How Life Is Played in Mexican Villages*. Suffice it to say in Oaxaca often a predominantly communal approach is taken when it comes to economic affairs.

Starting with the family unit, everyone works to fill their role and meet the collective needs of everyone else. The women traditionally provide a crucial structural role, taking on the relentless and arduous work to raise the children, maintain the household, cook, and provide support for the men. In terms of hours per day and effort expended, Oaxacan women run circles around the men. The men work, and their earnings provide all that is financially needed for everyone in the family, young and old. One does not have a retirement plan; one has children. Once you are too old to work, your children will work in your stead and continue to provide the family with the economic means for getting on. While I lie awake at night fretting about my ability to retire (spoiler alert - it won't happen!), folks who live in such families sleep soundly knowing that their family unit is strong and will provide for them and everyone else. As long as the family is growing and has everything that everyone needs to survive and get on, everything is going to be alright.

This attitude extends outward from the individual family into the whole town. Every red-blooded American has been taught since birth to abhor the dreaded C-word. Communists! American society has fundamentally defined its very existence as the antithesis of communism. In Oaxaca, similar ideals to communism play out under the guise of a different C-word - community.

In Oaxacan society, everyone in a community is obligated to look out for everyone else. No, not like a neighborhood watch. Financially. Given that most small towns are relatively poor and most people within them live a subsistence lifestyle, when one person starts to prosper the town comes knocking.

Let's say you start a burgeoning business selling mezcal to outsiders and making a tidy profit. Your neighbors may start bestowing you with honors. "We would love to give you the opportunity to be the patron of the yearly town festival." You get to buy the meat and make the booze for everybody. You may get the honor of paying for the band as well. "We want to dedicate a new school building to you and your family." Guess who gets to pay for it.

As grow your means, so too your obligations. Milton Friedman would be quick to point out that this disincentivizes the individual from innovation and production, and he would be right (I hate it when Milton Friedman is right.) This situation presents a mean Catch-22. You can work harder and make a profit, but your efforts benefit everyone else in your town as much if not more than they benefit you. For many, this makes living precisely within one's means much more attractive.

It would be easy to criticize the shortcomings of this system from the perspective of western capitalism. To those that would say that this economic system is 'wrong,' a few thoughts. First off, it's been working just fine for a several thousand years, thank you very much. Secondly, think now about your own retirement. Know that unless you come from a wealthy family, the only person looking out for you is you. The economic models of rural Oaxaca have their own distinct advantages despite their drawbacks.

Now let's flip back to mezcal but from a different perspective. You are a member of the upper-middle class from Mexico City. You know that mezcal has become a huge thing. It's the coolest thing in Mexico and quickly the coolest thing abroad. The idea strikes you to use your network of contacts, to venture off to Oaxaca, and to do what you do best—build a brand. You find an excellent quality producer of mezcal whose family has been producing spirits in a small town for three generations. What he and his family make is delicious, and you want to strike a deal.

What happens next is more often than not a collision of two different economic ways of thinking. The Chilango is thinking of his ability to make a profit, and the mezcalero is thinking about making ends meet for his family.

The landmine in this scenario is the concept of valuation. Regardless of the economic system, we humans have to agree on how much things are worth when we transact. Capitalism suggests that the easiest way to arrive at an answer to this question is for everyone to act as selfishly as possible. For those not deep in the econ world, I'm not making this up. This is the exact language used by Chicago School economists. If I selfishly want to sell something for the highest possible price, and my buyer wants to pay as little as possible, free-market capitalism concludes that we will arrive at the price that's the fairest for everybody.

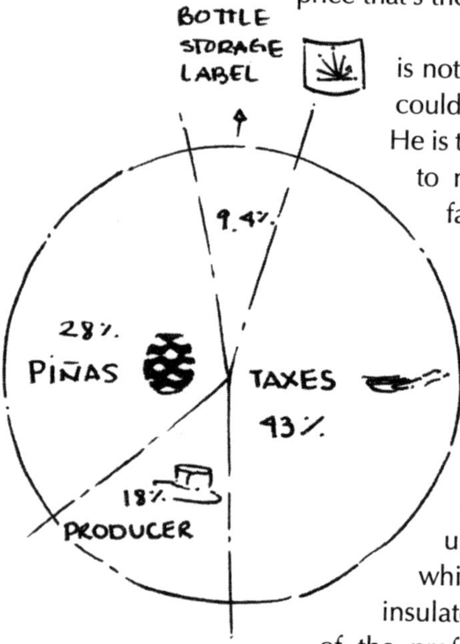

Returning to our mezcalero, he is not thinking how much he potentially could make from the sale of his wares. He is thinking about how much he needs to make to make ends meet for his family. Meanwhile, our city slicker wants to pay as little as possible and generate as much profit as they can.

This discrepancy is the single biggest hindrance to mezcal being an instrument of social justice or economic equalization. The rural and underserved communities in which mezcal is often produced are insulated from receiving a fair share of the profit generated due to a pervasive subsistence mindset and a cultural-economic disconnect. To make this a little less abstract, when you pick up a $50 bottle of mezcal made from agave espadín, somewhere around four of those dollars go to the family making it. Remember too that the agave from which the mezcal is made is not free, and must be paid for out of the amount that the producer receives.

The idea of fairness is highly relative, and you'll be hard-pressed to find a mezcal brand which does not quickly tout how well they do by their producers. I am in no way implying that these claims are in any way baseless or intentionally deceptive. Relationships between brands and producers vary, and each unique configuration is at the core of any given brand's values. At the extreme end of the spectrum, if you ask the palenquero how much they would like to be paid and then you pay them that amount exactly, it's hard to construe that you are taking advantage. In this scenario it's hard to imagine that the folks behind such a brand are unaware of the margins they are able to wring from the products that they sell. There are also a small handful of palenqueros operating outside of such situations who have created and found an opportunity for their own brands.

Brands are far from the sole drivers for the state of economic affairs. The certification process for a palenque is financially onerous, and the subsequent certification process for each batch of mezcal is both costly and arcane. The palenque certification alone costs well over $5,000 US dollars, which isn't easy to come by for small-scale producers in Oaxaca, Mexico's second poorest state. Add to this taxes, shipping costs, import costs, distribution costs, and retail markup, and you are looking at a $50 bottle of mezcal made from agave espadín.

What, then, is our proposed solution to this economic disconnect? When purchasing high-quality mezcal, we are voting with our dollars to support the efforts, the bulk of which emanate from the hands of the palenqueros, of the brands which we consume. Vexingly, it can often seem that a less-than-ideal amount of that money ends up in the palenquero's hands, and only very slowly are the positive economic effects of the mezcal boom trickling down to the ground level of the community.

It's at this point I regretfully admit that I do not have the answer. I certainly do not think it's the right thing to do to try to affect the culture of small producers from the outside, attempting to get them to subscribe more closely to our western capitalist ways. Even in a strictly subsistence-minded society producing mezcal provides an invaluable source of work and capital which sustains families and communities.

Let's walk through one possible way to tip the scales of fairness: place pressure on brands to lower prices. If the piece of the pie requested by the producers themselves is to remain small by their own volition, one way to make it more proportional to the other pieces of the pie would be to make the whole pie smaller. This—in addition to making many with a vested financial interest in mezcal very unhappy—would have a large number of side effects. I don't remember much from introductory econ, but I do know that if prices drop demand increases. If mezcal costs less, people will buy more mezcal. This would in turn increase production. This is a sure-fire recipe for an even bigger increase in mezcal sales than we've already seen in the recent past.

There are some huge disadvantages of this proposed solution which seem to make it largely untenable. For one, agave is a long-term crop and requires extensive forecasting to make sure that supply meets demand. If the market were to experience a sudden uptick in sales, a severe shortage of agave would be soon to follow. This pushes up prices of agave, which beget a need to pass that cost onto the end consumer. There is also the fact that these supply and demand forces affect consumer choices as well. If mezcal from agave tobalá were suddenly drastically less expensive, people would likely drink a lot more of it. This would translate into a genuine potential for ecological issues such as an acceleration of the inevitable overharvesting and disappearance of agaves in the wild, and the depletion of soil and water resources.

Placing pressure on brands to lower prices has another disadvantage which tips the scales even further to the unscrupulous. Those who pay their producers less stand to maintain a higher profit margin. It also incentivizes the use of agave either harvested early or of sub-par quality. By effectively increasing the price of less common agave types which are often harvested from the wild, it also increases the likelihood of agave poaching.

Lastly, this thought experiment highlights the complicated reasons behind the high prices of mezcal. Running a spirits brand is an expensive endeavor, and doing so internationally, doubly so. There are import taxes, storage and shipping concerns, and plenty of employees with different cost of living factors required to compete in a crowded marketplace. Distributors tack on roughly a third to the wholesale price, and retail marks things up from there. Mezcal is relatively unique as a category because regulatory costs on the ground in Mexico are disproportionately high. The CRM, operating effectively under the guise of being a not-for-profit organization, is responsible for a substantial chunk of the price increase between the producer and importer. Regulation of any DO spirit is essential to maintain quality and enforce standards, but the CRM as it currently operates falls victim to concepts which too often plague Mexican governmental affairs—influence-peddling and a pay-to-play mentality.

It seems the economic pressure angle is a non-starter. I can propose another, more moderate idea as a counter to our economic pickle. By carefully choosing which brands we support and whose products we consume, we can maximize the effects of voting with our dollars (or euros, or zloty). Even if a producer isn't the most exciting new thing on the market, or doesn't have the most handsome packing, nor offers some 'new' varietal we've never heard of, we can consciously reward those who are doing the best by the palenqueros and their communities.

It's extremely important to remember that size and equitability are not directly correlated. Just because a brand or operation is small does not mean that it is having the most positive impact on producer and community. There are many larger brands which use their financial backing to export quality products and foster long-term healthy relationships with their palenqueros. The longevity of these relationships is often a testament to their strength, equitability, and long-term impact. It's also impossible for any brand to exist outside the culture clash of economic perspective we talked about before. When facing cultural resistance to an individual profit motive, one does not need Evil Corporate Intent to have difficulty in insisting on paying their producers a premium. It's more likely a long and gentle process to have the sort of positive financial effect that capitalism teaches us to want to impart on those with whom we do business.

It can be argued that those communities in which folks are least capitalist-minded are often those most underserved with economic opportunity. This happens both through the cultural disconnect we've been looking at and also through systematic disenfranchisement on a governmental level. Laws in Oaxaca that give indigenous communities autonomy are also often imbued with subtle ways of keeping these same communities at arms length from state and federal investment. Even if only paying standard market rates, working with producers in these communities on their own terms can be an immeasurably important monetary driver for the overall financial health of the producer and their entire community.

We can also perhaps have the most significant impact by casting votes for regionally-owned and producer-owned brands. There are many reputable brands owned by folks from Mexico City, but it's hard to argue that they are as vested in the interests of the producing communities as the palenqueros themselves. Additionally, international operations with no vested interest other than profit loom large on the horizon. Upstart brands with questionable provenance already have and will continue coming to market. As much as I trust Faceless International Beverage Alcohol incorporated and their contemporaries as they quickly scramble to innovate in this new product space, they already seem to not be looking far beyond their bottom lines. Relationships in rural Mexico take time to build, and companies scrambling to build brands from scratch are doing so at the risk of being disconnected not only from the history and tradition of mezcal, but from that of Mexico as a whole.

As it seems, there is no short-term solution for long-term investment in mezcal producing peoples and communities. Putting money in the hands of a producer-owned brand puts money in the hands of those around them, and helps a community grow and prosper by their own hard work.

On tradition

Perhaps the most tantalizing thing about the world of mezcal is that it promises to offer the drinker a window into the past. The ideas of modernity have touched all spirits categories, and as we'll see that's ultimately a manifestation of the fundamental nature of human beings. Us humans tend to change and adapt things over time. Remember those big brains we were talking about? Adapting our behavior is a survival mechanism that's alive and well.

Despite its global emergence happening during the internet age, it's not uncommon to find palenques in which mezcal is produced by the same means, and in more-or-less the exact same ways it has been for several hundred years. The palate of mezcal exerts its charms in a very visceral way to audiences in search of the bold and the complex. Suffice it to say the liquid in the bottle stands on its own, easily justifying the newfound attention lavished on this ancient category.

We humans also tend to be suckers for a good story. The expensive French wine becomes all the better when we learn that the vines are over 100 years old and the winery has been passed down through countless generations. The category of mezcal has no shortage of personal and familial history. The liquid in the bottle is informed and elevated by the circumstance by which it got there.

When digging in as an outsider and searching to learn more about mezcal and its rich history, it doesn't take long until one encounters an incredibly problematic word. Tradition. What follows here is in no way an attempt to separate out what is or isn't traditional, but rather a series of open questions and a treatment of the idea of what tradition can mean to us as human beings.

The idea of tradition is as simple as it is familiar. It's the repetition of ideas, behaviors, techniques, or ways of living. Tradition can stretch back thousands of years or originate within recent memory. The most important traditions in our own lives are merely the ones that we chose to value highly. Historical importance, family involvement, and personal disposition all play a role in how important a tradition is and how likely it is to be passed on to the people around us or the generations beyond us.

In the case of inter-generational matters, the state of the world at large can play a role in the changing, tweaking, or eschewing of traditions. There are virtually no traditions in existence that exist absolutely unchanged from their inception, baring those which are extremely new. Tradition as an idea is a living, breathing thing, one which we have the good fortune of interacting with and contributing to in our lifetimes. How sad it would be to inherit tradition fully intact merely as a burden to pass on to the ages unembellished. We humans love putting our fingerprints on things, even if subtly.

When pondering on tradition as it pertains to mezcal we have to do our best not to generalize or round off the edges. What is traditional for one producer may be abhorrent to another. Traditions vary not only town-to-town but greatly person-to-person. Given that the process of making mezcal person-to-person is more similar than it is different—any non-fermenters in the house?—it's the minuscule details in the *how* of the production that affect the *what* of the result. Any factor of a palenquero's process may be influenced by intergenerational learning and personal preference alike. This is the small-picture of tradition.

The big-picture of tradition gets very problematic very quickly. To set a definition for an entire category is to run into near-constant exception. Name one defining characteristic of a cat. All cats have tails. Not all cats have tails. All cats have fur. Definitely, not all cats have fur. All cats have ears? Don't Google image search this one. There are some cats that don't have ears.

When pegging down even basic characteristics into Always and Never categories, we run into a hard time. At the end of the day, the Mexican government has taken a stab at defining what constitutes mezcal and has even gone as far as to quantify grades of mezcal based on production technique.

For all those who don't spend their time reading governmental regulations, the Consejo Regulador de Mezcal (CRM) is the governing body of the denomination of origin (DO) of mezcal. The organization is responsible for the creation of laws which govern the production of mezcal. Similar organizations exist throughout Mexico. The Consejo Regluador de Tequila (CRT) is the arbiter of all things tequila. Regulators craft sets of rules to govern Mexican DO products, known as Normas Oficial Mexicanas, or NOMs. A NOM is a rule book to which producers and brands must conform to have their products certified as belonging to that DO. If you want to put the word mezcal on the bottle, you have to play by the rules.

Every so often the CRM will question whether they should update the rules for mezcal production. The CRM will propose changes to the NOM and submit them for public review. After a period of discussion and feedback, the new proposed rules will either be put into play or discarded. Each NOM proposal is given a number by which it's referred. In 2017 a new NOM, NOM 070 was put into place. One of the biggest changes brought about by NOM 070 was the creation of three separate categories of mezcal.

While extremely well-intentioned, NOM-070-SCFI-2016, despite its catchy name, has not been received universally positive attention. Like it or not, it lays out specific criterion for different categories of mezcal based on production technique and equipment used. Think of each category as a set of minimum requirements, in which failing to meet one requirement rescinds the producer's ability to use that title. You must be this tall to ride.

The categories start out broadly with 'Mezcal.' Mezcal can be made with an earthen pit oven, above-ground tequila-style masonry ovens, an autoclave, or the dreaded diffuser. It also allows for roller mills for extraction and stainless steel column stills for distillation. The next rung up the ladder is 'Mezcal Artesanal.' Who doesn't want to be seen as artisanal these days? Mezcal Artesanal can be made with an earthen pit oven or an above-ground tequila-style masonry oven. It doesn't seem to explicitly preclude shredder roller mills, and can be made with any type of still. The highest echelon of mezcal according to the new Norma is 'Mezcal Ancestral.' The hallmark restriction of so-called ancestral mezcal is that it must be distilled in clay pot stills. Mezcales in this category must be roasted in earthen pits, and fermentation vessels are more tightly regulated.

	Roasting	Milling
Mezcal	· In earthen ovens · Masonry ovens · Autoclaves	· By hand · Tahona · Small milling machine · Wooden roller mill (trapiche) · Roller mills · Diffuser
Mezcal Artesanal	· In earthen ovens · Masonry ovens	· By hand · Tahona · Small milling machine · Wooden roller mill (trapiche)
Mezcal Ancestral	· In earthen ovens	· By hand · Tahona

Fermentation	Distillation
· In wooden tanks · Masonry tanks · Stainless steel tanks	· Pot stills · Continuous stills · Copper · Stainless column stills
· Soil or tree trunk · Stone · Clay pots · Animal skins	· With direct fire in copper stills · Clay pot still with clay head · Wood · Copper or stainless steel · May include agave fiber (or bagasse)
· Soil or tree trunk · Stone · Clay pots · Animal skins	· With direct fire in clay pot with clay head · Clay pot with wooden head · Which can contain agave fiber (bagasse)

There you have it, the definitive answer. Now we can all rest easy knowing firmly what makes one mezcal more connected to tradition than another. The regulations are undoubtedly well-intentioned, with the goal being making various mezcales easier to understand for the consumer. The problem lies in the seemingly arbitrary lines in the sand drawn between one category and another. The relatively low bar set for the Artesanal category is a bit of a head-scratcher. It seems larger, more industrial producers would very much like to be able to have their products considered to be artisanal. So too it's problematic to say that 'Ancestral' mezcal is only produced in clay. How about those whose ancestors have been distilling in copper for 300 years?

Annoyingly the categories may end up doing more to confuse consumers than to clear things up. It's a hard sell to say that clay is qualitatively 'better' than copper. No doubt that mezcales which fit the requirements to be labeled as ancestral will have added leverage to charge top dollar. Even further muddying the waters is the fact that not all producers choose to get certified in the first place. Some smaller producers are deciding to side-step government regulation altogether and sell what they personally refer to as mezcal under the label of *'destilado de agave.'* By avoiding the hoops needed to print the word mezcal anywhere on their label, smaller producers can avoid a whole host of hassles. Needing to produce in the geographically delineated areas, having to certify each batch, having to certify their palenque, needing to meet specific requirements for the chemical composition of their distillate, and even needing to bottle their product in Mexico can all be avoided by choosing the destilado de agave moniker.

The CRM and the Mexican government both seem satisfied in allowing these products to market as long as they don't use verbiage associated with the mezcal DO. Ultimately it is up to the consumer whether or not this label is seen as inferior or whether the allure of uncertified production makes the destilado de agave category even more sought after. Meanwhile, the ultimate authority on what any product is called lies not in the government's regulatory abilities, but in the nomenclature of the producer themselves. If they call it mezcal, I'm calling it mezcal too.

The ultimate goal behind the concept of creating a DO to regulate a product is twofold: to guarantee that copycat products produced in other places aren't going to encroach on a products name and identity, and to protect the quality and history of the product by enforcing strict production standards. One of the more controversial aspects of mezcal regulation is that the DO has at times indirectly forced small-scale, multigenerational producers to change their process to meet certification requirements. Chemical aspects of a certified mezcal are regulated, with caps imposed on things such as amounts of methanol, phenols, and acids present in the final product. If a producers' hundred-year-old process doesn't result in a spirit that meets these requirements, they can find themselves looking at one of two possibilities: change the process to conform or don't certify. As access to foreign markets is often contingent on certification, the more common result of restrictive quality standards is that more often than not producers are changing their process to conform.

Another factor that can cause a palenquero to change their process is the influence of the brand folks with whom they work. Folks who own brands, many of whom do not live in and are not from the areas in which their palenqueros live and work, fall broadly into two camps: interventionists and non-interventionists. At the extreme, non-interventionists seek to purchase spirits from established mezcal producers and do not ask them to change any details about their process or production. If the palenquero only makes 20 liters a month, the hardcore non-interventionist brand owner would not ask them to make more than that. One step beyond this perspective is helping a producer to scale up their production to produce more volume, but doing so carefully to allow the producer to achieve the results they always have.

Sadly, many brand folks fall firmly into the interventionist camp. Various reasons exist why a brand might ask their palenquero to produce differently: to conform to a house style, to be more broadly palatable or marketable, or simply because the brand owner prefers mezcales with a specific flavor profile. Sometimes the palenqueros products aren't of outstanding quality to begin with, and in those cases, it's somewhat relatable that a brand would intervene and work with the producer to change their wares. This situation still smacks of imperialism, but at least the argument could be made that without intervention the palenquero would never gain access to export markets. The flip side is that many producers of substantial quality are being made to change their production techniques to suit the whims of brand owners. There is a significant possibility that some product being touted to you as steeped in tradition or espousing a fifth-generation palenquero may very well have had the fingerprints of the maker smudged by the folks who put the label on the bottle.

Regardless of what it's called or how it is (or isn't) certified, questions surrounding tradition and quality remain. It should come as no small surprise that mezcal is a product and is meant to be consumed. The bulk of our focus in this book has been how outsiders relate to and understand the production and consumption patterns of the insiders. Mezcal for several hundred years has been largely a product focused on the relationship between consumer and producer, as any business enterprise should be. Mezcal has been primarily made in small villages for local consumption, and the resulting product is one we're lucky to get a glimpse of through the channels of international importers and folks who own brands. To say the highest quality or qualitatively best mezcal is the one that is the least touched by outsiders sounds on the surface like a convincing statement. When we venture down this path, we're including some anthropology in our way of thinking. We want to study and learn how this thing has been.

As said above, the mezcal consumed in small towns in Mexico is a result of a collaboration between the producer and their consumers. In a few places, this has manifested slightly differently than one would expect. Even coming from a cultural perspective in which one could debate the quality of one vodka or another by their relative 'smoothness,' we are quick to concede that mezcal is no shrinking violet. As a category, its ineffable charm certainly finds at least some of its roots in its unapologetically bold personality. In some producing communities, this has been taken a bit farther than in others.

In Miahuatlán producers often employ a piece of distillation equipment known as a *refrescador* or *refrescadera*. This is a trough on the outside of the head of the still through which cold water can be poured during distillation, increasing the efficiency of the still. When used for either one distillation or two, this ingenious innovation is often responsible for some incredible distillates. In other cases, it is occasionally used to make a product from one intentionally wide-cut pass. The fiery, potent, and rough-around-the-edges liquid may not be prized by its distillers, but it assures some in the local market that they're getting a product of sufficient strength. After all, we're not drinking this stuff for our health.

Consider also the case of mezcal amarillo. This situation is a bit of a chicken-or-the-egg scenario, but producers sometimes run clay pot stills with tin pans used in lieu of stainless steel or copper for cooling. Tin is reactive, and when the liquid condenses, it gains a yellow cast, which it maintains as it exits the carrizo and is collected. This copper-colored mezcal is seen by some locally as the only real way to know they're getting the 'good stuff,' even though it contains ample off flavors and is very possibly deleterious to human health. More so than beverage alcohol alone.

Supply chases demand, and a mezcal producer meets their consumers in the middle. Often times this results in a producer making the highest quality mezcal they can featuring their own personal stylistic hallmarks. Other times it means giving the consumers what they want whether the producer is a personal fan of the product or not. As the focus of some producers shifts from local to international markets, we too run the risk of getting exactly what we ask for.

We live in the age of YouTube, and the average human attention span sits well within sub-five-minute territory. One exciting aspect of mezcal is the vast diversity of the category. One can easily take in the breadth of American whiskey in a few focused hours. With mezcal, there is always another stone to overturn and another unique thing to explore —different varieties of agave, different production techniques, and vastly different production regions beget a mathematically daunting amount of possibilities to encounter.

Never have mezcal brands and producers been so focused on what the rest of the world wants mezcal to be. As we vote with our dollars for increasingly adventurous expressions of mezcal, brands and producers pay attention. Efforts have already been made to pander directly to international consumers predilection for novelty, and nowhere is this more apparent than in the category of mezcales de pechuga.

At its purest, the idea of a mezcal de pechuga is a celebration mezcal. The gist is that when celebrating a major life event, some palenqueros create a batch of mezcal to share with the community to fuel the festivities. In Oaxaca, this celebration mezcal is distilled twice, most often from agave espadín, and then macerated with other ingredients. This is where the artistic liberties come in, with the palenquero choosing which ingredients to use to flavor the mezcal. There are a host of possibilities, up to and including spices, seeds, nuts, dried fruits, and fresh *frutas criollas,* which are hyper-regional native fruits which usually only come in season for short periods of time. The mezcal is allowed to macerate and absorb the flavor of the ingredients, after which it is distilled for a third time. This is where the chicken comes in.

The origins and intentions of the next step of the process remain shrouded in mystery. Some producers hang a raw chicken breast inside the still during the third and final distillation. While there are some that swear the chicken breast has an ineffable yet profound impact on the resultant mezcal, I favor a more symbolic interpretation. A live chicken is a valuable resource in rural Oaxaca. One single chicken isn't enough to make sopa de pollo for a town of 150, so perhaps the use of the chicken in the distillation process is a way to ceremonially share your prize hen with the whole town.

Regardless of the origins, the result is a mezcal de pechuga. It ideally has the subtle flavors and aromas of both flavoring agents used and the agave itself. Mezcales de pechuga command top dollar, promising to let the drinker in on a particularly buoyant aspect of small-town Oaxacan life. The idea of making a celebration batch of mezcal with added ingredients isn't the sole territory of the state of Oaxaca, either. Other celebration mezcales can be found emanating from different producing regions of Mexico, each bearing a connection to local ingredients and traditions.

That being said, it's important to note that this type of tradition is not found in all mezcal producing communities, and where it is seen, it varies considerably in its application or the length of its traditional prevalence. As the emerging mezcal market chases after the tail of the consumer, there is no doubt in my mind that we will see this idea stretched far and wide. Adding additional ingredients to mezcal is very easy to accomplish, and if needing an example of manufactured scarcity, one needs to look no further than to the new American whiskey category. There are several brands bringing in 1000 liter lots of pechuga mezcal, and I've heard tell of a producer in Puebla who will make you a celebration mezcal out of ingredients that you bring him. Even flavored with your favorite type of tacos.

The judgment of the individual consumer must decide where the traditional aspect of this practice starts and ends. I don't know where tradition trails off into marketing, and it's doubtful that we'll ever have definitive answers as to whose rituals or 'traditions' are more traditional. For me, it's best to cast a critical eye and proceed with caution. I've always been quite the skeptic. For others, diving in and embracing some of the newer and more creative aspects of the world of mezcal may be just too enticing to pass up. Ultimately it's up to you to decide if it's worth $150 for a bottle of mezcal distilled lovingly with the inclusion of an expired iguana or tacos al pastor.

The State of Tequila

When considering the vast stylistic differences between tequila and mezcal, it is important to remember that tequila didn't end up Mexico's shining star of the international beverage scene by accident. Several producers shaped and molded tequila into its own category from the ground up, earning name recognition the world around in the process.

In the early 1800s, a small group of entrepreneurs set out to turn Jalisco's cottage industry of producing mezcal into an internationally viable business with growth potential. The mezcal being produced in Jalisco at the time shared stylistic hallmarks with the current categories of mezcal and raicilla, being produced with the same types of equipment in generally the same traditional ways.

When starting out on a new business endeavor, it's often wise to pay close attention to the competition and learn from their successes and mistakes. At the time, the world of luxury spirits looked somewhat similar to how it is today. French brandy and Scotch whiskey were sought-after import items in the New World. The Spaniards had come to Mexico with their brandy production in mind, and with them came copper pot stills ready to fire up. The only places in Mexico where grapes were, and still remain, viable, were mainly in the northwest. As such, the Spaniards sought alternative source material for their liquor-making pursuits. The traditions of agave-based pulque and Spanish brandy intertwined and thus, mezcal was born.

When later looking to fashion mezcal into an internationally viable industry, producers and distributors borrowed many pages from the playbooks of the other sought-after spirits from around the world. The defining characteristics of those benchmark world spirits were a soft, sweet palette and the fingerprints of oak aging. Little by little over the course of the 19th century, traditional mezcal producing techniques were eschewed in favor of modernity, productivity, and international amenability.

During the first 100 years of tequila history, producers slowly changed the production process to achieve the proto-industry's stated goals. Agricultural propagation of agave supplied the category's growing demand. As agriculture gained its footing, the varietal that would become known as tequilana Weber azul became the favored produce, as it's high sugar yield aided efficiency.

Pit roasting gave way to the stone oven, which is harder to build but much easier to load in and out. Hardwood for the roast was replaced by the most defining power source of the industrial revolution: steam. Gone was the smoky, roasty element created by fire. Tequila instead adopted an internationally-friendly clean flavor profile. Hand-mashing of agave was superseded by the tahona. Slow and laborious became quicker and more efficient. In 1857 Louis Pasteur began to unlock the secret life of yeast. In turn, producers learned to control their fermentation little by little to remove inconsistencies and eliminate the acidity and the funk created by a fully-spontaneous fermentation. Oak barrels were brought in and filled with finished blanco tequila, mimicking the aging seen in every other category of world-class luxury spirits.

By the late 1800s, the modernization efforts of the *tequileros* had resulted in a product more similar to the tequila of today than the mezcal traditions from which it evolved. At the 1893 Columbian Exposition in the city of Chicago, a *'mezcal de tequila'* from Casa Sauza won the 'world's best brandy' competition, firmly declaring that tequila had won a rightful place on the world stage of fine spirits.

Throughout the 20th century, the tequila industry never deviated from its intended mission of modernity and economic viability. This mindset carried forward, touching once again almost every aspect of the process. Farming many generations of agaves propagated by cloning has resulted in a monocultural crop of plants that aren't as genetically resilient as their forebearers. Some producers have opted to roast using large autoclaves, potentially speeding up the roasting process from days to hours. The tahona sees use in only a handful of contemporary distilleries, while large shredder rollers make the milling process more efficient for the majority of producers today.

The fermenter has seen its share of change as well. Wooden fermenters are exceedingly rare these days, with stainless steel providing a sanitary and controlled environment in which yeast can do their work. They're also very easy to clean and sanitize after the fermenter has been emptied. The yeast themselves are most often propagated from cultures in on-site laboratories, offering the greatest degree of control possible over the flavors that are—or perhaps more importantly aren't—created in fermentation. Additionally, the agave fibers are commonly removed during milling and never make their way to the fermenter. This allows for the use of mechanical pumps to transfer the fermented juices, or *mosto,* to the still but lessens the fibers' impact on the body and texture of the final product.

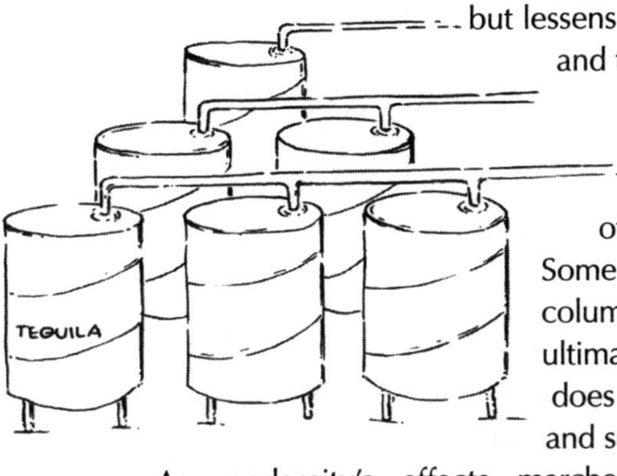

A majority of facilities continue to use pot stills, though some use stainless steel instead of copper for their construction. Some facilities have switched out for column stills, allowing the distiller ultimate control over what does and does not end up in the holding tank and subsequently the bottle.

As modernity's effects marched on, so too did tequila's international popularity. What was once an internationally-insignificant cottage industry was now bringing in some serious cash. With financial success comes partnerships, shareholders, international finance, and all kinds of complicated forces behind the scenes. The pressure to have an attractive bottom line has affected tequila in the modern era, resulting in shifting priorities and business practices.

One of the main challenges faced by the tequila industry surrounds its prize varietal of agave and the cultivation thereof. The long growth cycle of the blue agave, when compared to annual produce like corn, has resulted in resonating boom-bust cycles. Supply runs short, and demand stays the same. This means the price goes up, and growers rush to get plants in the ground given the current promise of a large paycheck. The only problem is that these plants do not come to maturity until upwards of 8 years after planting, at which point all the other agaves planted when prices were high also come to maturity as well. The results are plummeting prices and a glut in the market. Plants are left to rot in the fields as tequila producers reap the benefits of the rock-bottom prices for which they can purchase agave.

Sometimes during agave shortages producers can be tempted to harvest agave before the age of full maturity. While yield will be lower, immature agave still conforms to the legal production standards required by the Consejo Regulador de Tequila and can be used as a stop-gap. The temptation to do this is even further increased in producers using a diffuser for sugar extraction. Diffusers generally result in tequilas with more vegetal flavor profiles and slightly-too-young agave may blend right in.

The diffuser presents a whole host of problems when viewed through the lens of traditional production. For the sake of increasing sugar yield, producers make multiple sacrifices which affect the quality of the tequila produced. The sugars are not cooked until after they are removed from the agave fibers, and the cooking time trends towards shorter as well. The net result is a lot of green flavors and not a lot of characteristics of roast agave. The extraction process also involves a lot of nasties, including the spraying of the fibers with a solution of sulphuric acid to wring the sugars loose of the tough fibers.

If efficiency is the ultimate goal, then every step counts towards making the distillery more streamlined and thus more profitable. It's always a closed-door process, but sometimes additions are made to the ferment to help the process along. Urea is a chemical compound found in urine, and it's really good at getting yeast to get their hustle on. Yeast nutrients consisting of blends of various minerals are also very good at making sure that the yeast cells have everything they need to reproduce and do their thing. I'm not pointing any fingers, but these options are very much on the table for an economy-minded tequilero.

We don't have the time or the scope to dig into it here, but the relationship between tequila companies and small agave growers are extremely problematic. It's hard to imagine a better treatment exists on the subject than Sarah Bowen's *Divided Spirits*. If you haven't already, you should definitely check it out. It can't be said that it directly affects the quality of tequila available, but any overview of tequila's more unsavory aspects would be incomplete without its mention.

Lastly exists what I would argue is the single greatest impediment to the quality of the tequila market at large, the laws governing tequilas production, the Norma Oficial Mexicanas. The NOMs allow for certain categories of additives to comprise up to 1% of the total volume of the finished product. The categories of additives approved are: 1) caramel coloring 2) wood extracts to normalize for aging 3) glycerin and 4) flavoring agents approved for use by the Mexican government. Let's break this down one by one.

Caramel coloring is fairly common for use in spirits. Scotch whiskey would lack its deep amber tones, and amari wouldn't exude their murky charm without it. The inclusion of caramel color isn't out of place in the world of spirits, but it does mean that it's impossible to tell if the color of that extra anejo was imparted by its aging or bolstered by some post-production magic.

Wood extracts aren't super sexy, but they're not unheard of additives in the world of quality spirits. Cognac as a category is both highly secretive about and stylistically dependant on the use of wood extracts to provide tannin and bolster the aging process. Again, this isn't out of place in the world of spirits, but it is a bit less common than the use of caramel coloring.

Glycerin as an additive can be used to bolster a tequila's body. It has a very distinctive texture and can be picked out by the trained palate. Mouthfeel in spirits comes mostly from residual sugar and lipid content that float their way through the still, as we talked about earlier. It's either sweet, oily, or both. Any texture that can't be ascribed to one or the other starts to raise suspicion that maybe a producer puts a bit too much emphasis on 'smoothness.'

Finally is the elephant in tequila's room. The flavoring agents in question are literally any which have been approved for human consumption by the Mexican government. This includes both natural and artificial flavors. One percent by volume is a tremendously high ceiling given the incredibly potent food flavoring agents available. Anything from vanilla extract to artificial cotton candy flavoring could be added to a tequila by its producer.

The use of natural and artificial flavoring agents in the category of tequila creates a murky world full of suspicion. For those following along, these additives and extracts can be added to any product within the tequila category, very much including Tequilas labeled as "100% agave." Upon tasting any tequila, one has no choice but to guess at the sources of the flavors in the glass. Tequilas available on the market range from the virtually untouched to the artfully altered to the heavily modified. There are no labeling requirements and no public formula disclosures. The consumer ultimately has no idea what they're drinking, and no producers will cop to adultering their product no matter how heavy-handed the application of artificial coconut flavoring.

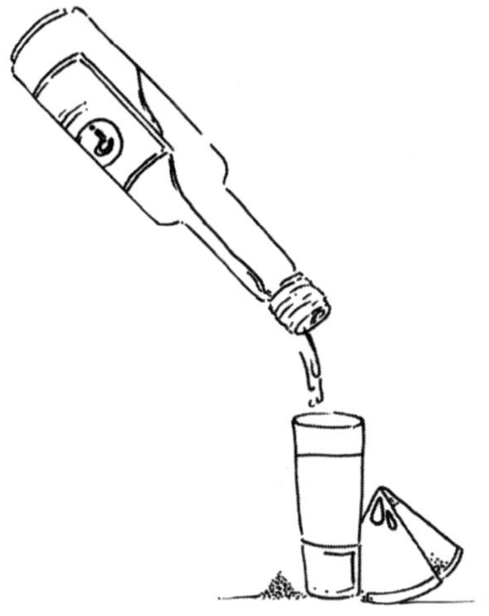

Let's take a step back and do a thought experiment. Brand A is a mid-sized tequila producer hoping to grow their share of the market. They're in direct competition with Brand B, who is more established and has a bigger piece of the pie. Brand A is conceptually committed to producing a tequila that is honest and straightforward. They've never used additives to change or modify their product. Brand B, however artfully uses a proprietary blend of flavors and a small amount of glycerin for texture. They've spent obscene amounts of money dialing in their flavor profile and doing focus groups to make sure their product is exactly what their target consumer wants.

What's Brand A to do? Their competitor creates a heat-seeking missile aimed directly at their consumer's pocketbooks. How are they to compete? The way that the tequila industry has been structured, it's extremely hard for producers to compete without playing the additive game. The result has been an even murkier market and contemporary products that taste drastically different than juice from the same producer from years back.

For me, it's a scenario where more often than not everyone cheats and no one wins. It's a process and a resultant product that's drastically out of sync with contemporary consumer demand for wholesomeness and transparency. Until the firewall between consumers and the process of tequila's creation is eliminated, the category of tequila will disproportionately reward those large producers doing things the wrong way and hinder those who refuse to play the game.

The Future

When we set out on our journey, I promised that I was going to give you information that you were expected to do something with. We've talked about the agave plant and how people learned to live alongside it, the process of making booze from it, the science behind its fermentation and distillation, and the economic realities impacting the lives of its producers. We've seen how tough it can be to talk about tradition, and we've explored the reasons that tequila as a category makes me sad. Now we've come to the point where we get to ask the big questions. What can we as consumers and bar-folk do about the growth of an industry to which we're at arms-length at best?

Here we are at the first stop on our 'what's next' journey towards the future. Copious consumer and bartender education is no doubt a crucial component of the future of agave spirits. I'll address the bar professionals first.

Question everything. All of your reps, many of whom are acquaintances or friends, will be relaying information to you with the intent of casting the best light possible on their employer's brands. You wouldn't tell your guests if your fresh lime juice was placed into painter's buckets that are set on the kitchen floor occasionally. When in a sales role we only share the information which shows the best of our wares. Besides, the lids were on those buckets the whole time. Also, many of the sales folks won't have spent any substantial time on the ground at the palenques with whom the brand works. They may not be privy to the inner workings of the organizations which employ them. Nothing is wrong with this, but it also means they're sometimes approaching you with an incomplete picture of the operations they represent. The knowledge gap is yours to fill. Not your homie's. Yours. The info you need won't be found on a tasting mat or in a pdf sales sheet. Talk to trusted sources and cross-check what they say with others.

Consumers, you, not the bar folk, are the ultimate drivers of the mezcal market. Your friendly neighborhood bartender has only the best intentions and is in no way ever trying to mislead you. Remember, though, that some of the information they're providing you is likely third-hand. Not everyone has the extreme good fortune to travel to visit their producers and investigate how they work and what they make. Know too that there's a lot of information competing for the mental bandwidth of the contemporary bar professional. Some of us even have lives outside of work. Just understand that the way booze is sold is potentially problematic, and never hesitate to pressure your bartender if your own research leads you to feel they're working with a low quality or unscrupulous producer.

For consumer and bartender alike, there is one shining source of truth and clarity in the world of mezcal: the products themselves. Pay attention any time someone shares with you the process by which they taste spirits - over the past decade my tasting procedure has changed annually, as I find what works best for me. As you gain confidence in your process, be analytical and share your notes with others. While developing consensus is never the goal, you'll learn from others as they learn from you.

There's a reason we spent some serious time on distillation in this book: by knowing more about the process and technical inner-workings, you can infer more from what you taste in the glass. There will come a time, and it will be sooner rather than later, that someone will try to sell you on a low-quality product. There will be something set in front of you in which a production fault will be shared as a selling point, an asset. Mezcal's big personality and rustic nature can naturally encompass aromas and flavors which in all other spirits would be considered faults. 'It's so *funky,* and so *different.'* One must remember that there's empirically good funky and weird, and empirically bad as well. Constantly striving to have a good grasp on overall quality is the only defense we have against being sold bad juice. There's already some on the market and be assured there's even more on the way.

Having a solid palate and a grasp on how to taste will also allow us to better understand why and how products change over time. Wild fermentation and ever-changing conditions mean that consistency in mezcal is a very loose idea, but it's more likely than not there will come a time when a former producer of notable quality will begin cutting corners for economy's sake.

Everything we've covered so far is pretty high-commitment. What if you don't have an extra five hours a week to contribute to analytical blind tasting? Find voices and palates you trust and listen to what they share with you. You can extrapolate from their effort and help to amplify their message. Think of it like voting. I don't really have the patience or free time to research the best candidate for Metropolitan Water Reclamation District, but if I have a network of politically-minded friends with whom I generally agree, I can trust and help to amplify their well-researched positions.

The next major area of focus for the future is accountability. We must ask brand folks to share with us the absolute maximum amount of information possible. Know who makes your mezcal, and where. How large the batches are. When it was made. The palenquero's relationship to the brand. Information about their family.

We live in a strange, and somewhat annoying, time. Accessibility to information has meant that things that were once proprietary have become common knowledge. Decreasingly is knowledge a self-sufficient asset, and increasingly we expect knowledge and action from the others around us. While it's a tough ask to root around through a brand's accounting ledgers, the distribution of income and profits is the single biggest human concern when it comes to brand responsibility. How much of that $120 bottle of tobalá ends up in the hands of the producer. It's a tough ask, but the more pressure placed by consumers, the more likely we will gain access to such information and be able to use it to gain insight into a given brand's commitment to social responsibility.

On the subject of accountability, bartenders, if you are able to, visit your producers. Get your feet on the ground and ask questions. Sniff around. Take pictures of everything. See the operations of the folks you work with and perhaps, more importantly, those you don't. Seeing with your own eyes and being inquisitive are the single best ways to gain a better grasp about with whom you should be working and with whom you perhaps shouldn't. Compare what you've seen where, and never be afraid to ask the same question of multiple different people to see not only their production but their philosophy.

On that note, don't believe every rumor you hear. It's not uncommon to hear off-hand comments about other producers, and it's always worthy of doing due diligence to see if the accusations are fact or mere allegation. The world of mezcal is notably political, the business of mezcal is a pursuit into which many people have poured an awful lot of their passion and pride. It never hurts to sniff around a bit before repeating allegations against others as absolute fact.

There's no greater way to assure social accountability than to support producer-owned brands. There are those who would call their operations co-ops, while the reality seems far more transactional. When I go to the grocery store and purchase produce, the person at the check-out counter and I aren't part of a cooperative organization. I'm their customer. There's nothing wrong with a brand purchasing and bottling spirits from a palenquero, but it's rare to find a true co-op structure to the arrangement.

A few legitimate producer cooperatives exist, and it's a model that seems to have demonstrated viability. There are also a handful of family-owned brands which offer the promise of focusing the economic benefit of mezcal's meteoric rise into the smaller towns in which the producing family lives. For the time being, buying a family-owned or community-owned brand is the more sure-fire way to know where the money from your purchase ends up.

We also must remember that accountability extends into the realm of sustainability. There are a whole host of areas about which we must worry. The area most frequently addressed is that of agave agriculture. Despite concerted planting efforts of what are currently effectively 'wild' agave varietals, overharvesting in the wild can have a devastating impact on the biosphere of these incredible plants. To help mitigate this, we as consumers must focus our indulgences on agave varietals that have less of an ecological impact.

Drink more espadín. *A. Karwinskii* varietals are a bit less prized and grow a bit faster than others. Agave *convallis* is so hard to work with that large populations exist in the wild relatively undisturbed. *Agave Cupreata* and *Agave Salmiana* are abundant along the Pacific coast and in San Luis Potosi, respectively. I'm not saying to abstain from consuming other 'wild' varietals, but think of it this way: you don't go to the steakhouse and eat prime rib every day. Drinking more espadín or cupreata on everyday occasions and focusing on indulging in other varietals more infrequently can have a big impact.

There are also many other aspects that are often forgotten about when it comes to sustainability: effluent treatment and heat pollution of streams and rivers. Potable water usage and depletion. Land use and soil management. The vast amounts of spent agave fibers left over after production. All of these are very real problems that must be dealt with on a producer-by-producer and a brand-by-brand basis. Ask brand folks about not only their agave planting and conservation efforts, but where the wastewater from the palenquero's operation ends up. Right now these are relatively small concerns, but in the aggregate they can have real negative effects on a producer's community directly.

We've saved the most problematic piece of the puzzle for last. The Mexican government's regulatory efforts of mezcal and related spirits have run the gamut from concise and effective, to ham-handed, to politically corrupt and morally bankrupt. The mezcal DO is exclusionary, and some of the chemical regulatory standards it contains feel arbitrary. Many producers who for generations have been producing mezcal have found themselves no longer able to use the category name to describe their wares. Conversely, dissimilar traditions have been lumped together and held to the same set of rules and regulations.

At this stage the mezcal DO is well established. We find ourselves in a position where we are unable to put the bullet back in the gun, even if we wanted to. Disenfranchised producers of mezcal in Estado de México and Jalisco will only get to use their preferred name for their product if the DO expands its purview, as it seems to intend to do. At best, the DO can create and enforce regulations which would guarantee a minimum level of quality for the category, and could provide economic and environmental guidance to enrich communities and to safeguard the environment. This would double down on both the image and the reality of mezcal being a world-class craft spirit. The DO could ultimately end up being an instrument by which the rich tradition of mezcal is preserved and the voices of those who produce it are amplified on a world stage.

The current reality of the DO is a bit less sunny, and its potential for drifting further away from potential lofty goals is very real. The DO can just as easily find itself as the gatekeeper of those who do and do not have access to the booming mezcal export market. It can operate as an increasingly for-profit enterprise and a political actor. The regulations imposed on producers which purport to guarantee quality can also be configured to codify unwholesome practices and unsavory products. One needs to look no farther than tequila to see that strict rules can sometimes be used to circumvent quality rather than to protect it. The fees the DO charges act as a form of producer tax, and also as a barrier to market for those with the least access to capital. To peg me as wholly pro-regulation would be to overlook all of these glaring downsides, both present and potential, to the concept of regulation.

I do, however, favor a big-tent approach to the category of mezcal, but with the increased ability to recognize regional peculiarities and traditions. There is no reason that the DO couldn't recognize variable or more stringent standards for specific regions if the producers of that region agree upon them. If all producers in Santa Catarina Minas agree that their tradition is to use clay pot stills, they should be able to enshrine that tradition in the protection of the law. There's no reason they shouldn't be able to create a sub-classification which sets forth rules for the production and labeling of mezcales made there.

There are those who have suggested that abolishing the DO and de-regulating the word mezcal are the cure to what ails the category. I do believe firmly that the DO needs drastic reform, but I'm not an abolitionist. I believe that the key to a high-quality and reputable spirit category is stringent regulation and high standards. While I have no problem trusting a generations-old palenquero to produce products which are unadulterated and high quality, I don't extend such faith to George Clooney and his upstart multinational confederates. Some form of independent, strict, and uncompromising regulation is needed to prevent the long, slow slide from a category thoroughly exemplary of the promise of craft and tradition into a sad, stodgy tequila 2.0.

Further Reading:

- Agaves & General Mezcal Production:

  Agaves Yuccas and Related Succulents, Mary & Gary Irish, Timber Press, c 2000

  Mezcal, Our Essence, Yuri de Gortari and Edmundo Escamilla, Consejo Mexicano de Productores de Maguey Mezcal, A.C., c 2009

  The Anatomy of Mezcal, Dr. Ivan Saldaña Oyarzábal, ExpressIt Media, LLC, c 2013

- Fermentation:

  Yeast - The Practical Guide to Beer Fermentation, Chris White with Jamil Zainasheff, Brewers Publications, c 2010

  The Art of Fermentation, sandor Ellix Katz, Chelsea Green Publishing, c 2012

- Distillation:

  Fermented Beverage Production Second Edition, Andrew G.H. Lea & John R. Piggott, Springer Science and Business Media, LLC, c 2003

  Unit Operations of Chemical Engineering Fourth Edition, McAbe, Smith, & Harriott, McGraw Hill, c 1985

- Economic Sociology of Rural Oaxaca:

  The Other Game - Lessons from How Life Is Played in Mexican Villages, Phil Dahl-Bredine & Stephen Hicken, Orbis Books, c 2008

About the Author

Jay Schroeder has dedicated his career to agave and cocktail culture, working exclusively with agave products for years to become one of the preeminent authorities on Mexican spirits in the industry. Schroeder's history with agave spirits includes running the beverage program for Rick Bayless's top restaurants Frontera Grill, Topolobampo and Xoco; launching the award-winning Mezcaleria Las Flores in Chicago's Logan Square neighborhood and most recently running the beverage program as a partner at Logan Square's acclaimed restaurant Quiote and adjacent mezcaleria Todos Santos.